A BLACK FIRST

Peter E. Carter

AAPPEAL

ISBN-13: 978-1-7336455-3-9

Cover Design by Purdue Designs, Macon, GA. www.tpurdue.com

Publisher: AAPPEAL, LLC, Cranberry Township, PA www.eac-aappeal.com

A BLACK FIRST

Chapter 1. The Beginning 1

Chapter 2. Uptown Manhattan 7

Chapter 3. Citizenship 15

Chapter 4. Brooklyn 19

Chapter 5. Regis High School and My Mother 29

Chapter 6. CYO Day Camp, Coney Island, Brooklyn 39

Chapter 7. The Bronx and Fordham University 45

Chapter 8. Job Hunting and My First Job 53

Chapter 9. The Funeral, the Wedding, and the Birth 63

Chapter 10. Moving in and Moving on, and
Another Birth 67

Chapter 11. Another Journey Begins:
Bedford-Stuyvesant and Wyandanch 73

Chapter 12. Meanwhile 81

Chapter 13. Gauger Middle School: Newark, Delaware . 85

Chapter 14. The New Jersey Ride Begins:
Franklin Middle School, Metuchen 93

Chapter 15. Irvington, New Jersey:
Its Board, Its Government, and Its Essence 101

Chapter 16. Roselle, New Jersey: My First
Superintendency 107

Chapter 17. New Jersey Department of Education:
Essex County Office 109

Chapter 18. A Mental Pause 121

Chapter 19. The Return to Irvington, New Jersey 127

Chapter 20. Just Before the End 143

Chapter 21. Ringwood, New Jersey: The Final Frontier
.... 147

Chapter 1

The Beginning

It all started for me aboard a Pan American airplane on its way from Trinidad, British West Indies, to New York City. Actually, it really started some two years prior to that, but my own recollection takes me back to being two years old on an airplane reading from what was called a British primer (in today's jargon, a reading textbook for the prekindergarten years). Several White people on the plane were giving my mother dollar bills in recognition of her or my phonetic accomplishment. I was later to learn why: At the time in America, Negro children of any age could not read or read very poorly. I was like a circus act for these White folks, something different for them, something unique—a colored child not only talking but also reading.

As I recall, it was cold so probably wintertime here in the U.S. of A. in New York City, Harlem; 118th Street. It was where my grandmother resided in a multiroomed apartment on the third or fourth floor, several of which rooms were rented to *lodgers*, as they were called. She was the landlady, as I would come to learn, and every week, they came down the hall to her living quarters and gave her money, and she gave each of them a piece of paper which I was told was called a *receipt*. There were about three lodgers, so the logical question is, where did my mother and/or I sleep or even be? All I recall is two things about this situation: I slept on a love seat, and my mother and her mother were constantly speaking at each other in loud tones, and I mean constantly. It was my grandmother who had brought us here to America.

Let me tell you as much as I recall about my grandmother at this point in my life. She was like a Queen of Harlem, a midwife working at a place called Harlem Hospital, the night shift no less. Grandma walked the streets to and from wherever she had to be, never molested, never mugged, never even verbally assaulted. The men who lurked in the streets always tipped their hats with a pleasant, "Good evening, Mrs. S." Uptown New York City in the late 1940s was urban and dangerous, and an economic entity unto itself. So, Grandma had her legit professional medical gig, her lodgers, and—of course—she played *the number*.

The journalistic lifeline of New York City was a newspaper called *The Daily News*. Its readers had little interest in the news of politics, crime, advice to the lovelorn, or even the Yankees, although the paper was read from the back (the Sports section) to the front. The essence of the rear of the publication was the horseracing results and the dollars taken in at the track. There is this thing called *the handle*, the total take in dollars for the day, and the last three numerals of the handle (usually an eight-figure number) was the daily *number*. I recall seeing quite a bit of money coming and going with regard to the number. All you had to do was predict twenty-four or so hours in advance what the last three numbers were going to be. This gambling practice was illegal, of course, but thousands of Black people played the number daily, and thousands of Black people lost their food and rent money and welfare check proceeds weekly. It was Harlem's own lottery, decades before the State realized what a goldmine existed in guessing three numbers either straight or in combination. My grandmother was a number lady, and she and her neighbors stored large sums of money in their bosoms and/or brassieres. Yes, I was quite the observant little boy, who asked very few questions. Children back then were not permitted to ask questions, and we didn't for fear of the physical pain which could be endured as a result of actually speaking to an adult (*grown folk*, as they were called). But back to my grandmother, who was feared by most who crossed her many paths. She was not a very nice person, so I never understood how she could exercise a positive bedside manner and deliver so many babies a week. Also, she liked money; she liked money a lot. She liked money so much that, because my mother never obtained gainful employment as an immigrant from the West Indies, she threw the two of us—her daughter and grandson—out of her tenement apartment since my mother had no money for rent. Yes, rent for the small area of the apartment which we inhabited with her.

I remember only too well being with my tearful mother (she was tearful all too often during our days at Grandma's abode) outside the tenement building with all our belongings. A small pick-up-type truck drove by then stopped, and the driver asked, "Can I take you folks some place?" I was six years old, I think, when my mother and I and a total stranger loaded up a vehicle and headed further uptown to 148th Street to a one-room apartment on the third floor of a house owned by another Black woman with tenants. It is here where the story of yours truly really begins, in a community called Morningside Heights and Sugar Hill. It was between St. Nicholas and Convent Avenues across from a bar and grill, and an uphill walk to Amsterdam Avenue and north to 153rd Street and St. Catherine of Genoa Parochial School.

The daily walk was refreshing, even in the rain or snow. Mobility during the cold weather was a bit of a challenge since my mother insisted on bundling me up like an Amazon delivery, decades before anyone had ever heard of

Amazon. Needless to say, I would lose a glove now and then, which often resulted in my having to wear mismatched items to keep my hands warm. There was so much to observe on my daily walk to and from school. The houses were magnificent from the outside; I could only imagine the interiors and thought about one day living in one of them or something similar. It was a dream reinforced daily, but thankfully never to come true. I politely acknowledged the owners I passed along the way with a tip of my cap to the women on their stoops, although as I reflect back, they were probably merely tenants themselves, or even maybe "The Help."

Chapter 2

Uptown Manhattan

Somehow, it is the first day or maybe the Friday before the first day of school. Perhaps, too, now is a good time to interject some other numbers into the narrative. It is the late summer of 1950, and I am six years old. I have no idea what happened in the intervening years with regard to my upbringing and/or any formal education. I recall attending a nursery school of some kind for a while so that my mother could go to school at the Y [YMCA/YWCA] to learn secretarial skills such as shorthand and typing. There were times for whatever reason that I was present in that Y classroom observing something called Gregg shorthand, my first glimpse of what appeared to me to be a foreign language. Of course, I learned some it; I found the symbols interesting and exciting, said symbols having been replacements for words and phonetics. But we need to get back to that nursery school for just a brief moment in order to share an item of my early education. For the record, all of my three Rs were infused in me by my mother, who somehow even found the *Dick and Jane* reader for me and countless, and I mean countless, arithmetic books and problems. Oh, did I mention that my mother claimed to have been a school teacher back in Trinidad where I was conceived and born? So, from birth to six, I had the best schooling possible with a one-on-one 24/7 teacher, which I assure you did not stop at six years of age.

Of course, there are some things one's mother does not teach a son, and thus the nursery school piece. This particular nursery school had a single toilet facility for the boys and girls. I recall there being an even mix of the genders, and perhaps fifteen of us in the group of five-year-olds (or maybe we were even four-year-olds). I recall, too, our "curriculum" was full of arts and crafts and papier-mâché projects. Lots of flour and water and newsprint in the schoolroom and unisex bathroom. The place was a bit of a mess, actually, but it was a place for me to be while my mother was not at home. There was a little girl whose name escapes me, and just as well, as you will agree as you read further, in the classroom of whom I became quite fond, and she fond of me, I suppose. There came a point in time when we both found ourselves in the restroom together (her idea, I think) and I was given a lesson in the female anatomy. She proceeded to pull up her dress, pull down her white underwear (back then, all girls' underwear was either white or pink), and thus show and expose herself to me. Since it was clear that she was missing something which I had, the question of "going to the bathroom" arose, to which she replied, "It comes through here," pointing to her general vaginal area, and then proceeded to urinate from a standing position into the toilet bowl while reciting the word, "See!" The entire incident, if you could call it that, probably lasted no more than two minutes or so, for surely we would have been missed by the teacher or whatever the title was of the person in charge of this place. So papier-mâché and Pee are the only memories I have of any formal preschool, and I do not recall ever seeing my five-year-old anatomy instructor and guide ever again after our engagement in the unisex toilet. Oh, yes, I told my mother (no, not the nursery school teacher), whose response I shall always remember, "Girls and ladies must stoop when they go to the bathroom, son." This was to be the first of many admonitions from Miss Carter to her son, Peter, on the topic of sexual and coed relations. However, it was the only time she (or I, for that matter) ever spoke on the topic of my nursery school boys/girls' bathroom escapade.

Now to return to formal schooling and our trip to St. Catherine's for what could be termed the *registration process*. Somehow, my mother had arranged to meet with the principal, a member of the order of Sisters of Mercy, one Sister Mary B. I came to learn later that the pupils and even staff referred to her as *B-meana*, an apt nickname, but not applicable in my case. For some reason, my mother brought with her samples of her son's schoolwork from the months of learning under her tutelage. Sister examined the exhibits and chatted with me. During the brief conversation, based clearly on the data she had examined, she asked me if I wanted to be a priest. I did not know much about the priesthood at the time, but somehow I guess in her mind it was related to intelligence and academic performance. Let's leave that theory alone for now, especially since my response to Sister Mary B was, "I don't think so." The principal assigned me to a first-grade classroom to which I reported the first day of school with my clean white shirt, blue trousers, and something around my neck known henceforth as a tie. The second day of school, I was placed in second grade. I was six years of age, and thus the youngest child in the class, a fact which remained for the next years of my elementary, secondary, and higher education experience. The teacher's name was Sister Mary C, an absolutely attractive female hiding in a nun's habit. There were positive interactions for the year I was destined to spend at this school, located across the street from a cemetery with a medieval aura and two blocks from the Museum of the American Indian. My grades, as I recall, were outstanding, the lowest of which may have been a 96 on a spelling test, to the utter chagrin of my mother, whose norm was always excellence and perfection. Sister Mary C really liked me, and I liked her. I was given all types of little chores on a daily basis. My first year at a real school was terrific except for one interesting factor.

Trinidad was a British colony when I was born and thus the "educated" natives spoke with a distinctly British accent, as did their offspring. Thus, my classmates, who also liked me, I think, would comment, "You talk funny." Realizing that I was already visually different, it dawned on me (as a young political animal) that the accent had to go. The next years were spent in developing an American accent, much to the anger and disappointment of my mother. However, survival was essential, and the eradication of my British and Caribbean tones was a priority in my mind. Circumstances of geography assisted in this transition since we moved to Brooklyn for my third grade of schooling.

That first year of school in the second grade was not without its nonacademic challenges. Living in one room and sharing a bathroom with another tenant was quite a feat. Having only two shirts and one pair of "good" trousers was a problem, especially since I liked to run a lot and would fall, and thus rip that one pair of pants which had to be immediately sewn. My shirt had to be washed daily so it would be clean and dry two days hence. Keep in mind we had no washing machine or dryer—just a window sill with sunshine. We had an iron, as I recall. My mother had to scrub the toilet seat before use, making it imperative that I announce my intentions to her in advance. The kitchen was also shared, but it appeared that the other tenant on the floor did not cook but merely boiled water occasionally. Living in this illegal multiple dwelling was a gentleman who (at least) weekly came home quite intoxicated, collapsed at the base of the stairs, and had to be helped to his living quarters by members of the New York City Police Department. There were very few other children on 148th Street, so I played outside with myself most days and weekends once chores and schoolwork had been completed. On the corner was the bar and grill that I mentioned previously, easily viewed from the window of our room. Every weekend on a Friday or Saturday night, a patron was arrested for some reason or another. The arrest process was brutal as the cops forced the prisoner's hands behind his back in order to apply the handcuffs, while both parties uttered some pretty vulgar words, followed by the stuffing of this human being into the police car. The cops were White; the prisoners were Black. I knew I never wanted to be arrested, and never was.

My mother had somehow arranged medical services for me at St. Clare's Hospital in midtown Manhattan and I visited a pediatrician fairly regularly. I guess I was "sickly," even though I rarely missed school. The doctor, whose Italian surname I do recall but shall not mention, was terrific. We liked each other a lot and he was particularly taken with my speech and ability to move rhythmically. One visit out of nowhere, he announced that I had contracted tuberculosis (TB). He and other doctors treated me successfully for this serious ailment, allowing me to reach age 7. That one room we lived in nearly killed me. Yes, in addition to the conditions I have already described, there were cockroaches and mice living among us.

Miss Carter had done sufficient research into the system to have applied for public housing so that we could move from this place which was killing both of us. My mother had developed a stomach ulcer which would eventually lead to other more complicated medical matters. She often had bouts of regurgitation of her digested food. The doctors at the clinic seems baffled as to how to treat this situation, given the fact that such incidents kept recurring.

I recall several trips on the subway to Rector Street during her quest for public housing and for other legal or bureaucratic matters. She was successful and was assigned by the Housing Authority to a one-bedroom apartment at 218 Bond Street in Brooklyn to which we moved sometime in the summer of my seventh year on earth, my fifth year in America.

Chapter 3

Citizenship

On one of our trips to downtown Manhattan on the subway, my mother and I found ourselves in a large courthouse with many people of different dialects but similar hues who were about to be sworn in as naturalized American citizens. My mother was there to also pledge allegiance to the United States of America, land of the free, home of the brave, with liberty and justice for all. Adult immigrants of the Caucasian persuasion, including those with young children, were happily welcomed into the chambers in anticipation of the proceedings. As my mother and I attempted to go through the doors, a White man in a blue uniform with some sort of a badge (I knew he was not NYPD; I had seen dozens of them in my few years in the city) stopped her and stated emphatically that I had to remain in the lobby area—something about children not being allowed. That man in the blue uniform had just made the worst mistake of his career as a security officer. At the exhale of his final syllable, Miss Carter pointed out in her well-defined British West Indian accent in a quite audible tone that other children were already in the courtroom and they happened to be White in hue. She made it quite clear that in preparation for her citizenship, she had studied and learned that all men were created equal, etc., so how could it be that her son who was colored was being denied access, unlike the sons and daughters of the others who were White. She made it extremely obvious that this act of discrimination at the occasion of the granting of citizenship was certainly contrary to the nature of the proceedings. I do not recall whether she opted to use any appropriate adjectives directly toward this White authority person, but quite shortly after her initial exhortation, there was supervisory intervention, and yours truly was permitted to see his mother sworn in as a United States Citizen.

Welcome to racist America, Miss Carter and Peter, welcome! Even though I was aware of racial differences as I advanced as a little boy, nothing so far had been as stark as this affront at a federal event in a federal building. "One nation," ("under God" was not included yet), "indivisible with liberty and justice for all" did not quite define what happened that morning. What the incident did teach me was to never allow anyone to treat me differently or unlawfully just because I was a Negro. I also learned what a force to be reckoned with my mother was.

I sort of knew, but I thought it was only toward her little son, who often felt (and I mean felt— leather hurts) the strength of that woman when her rules—and there were many—were not followed. At the end of the general swearing-in, the new citizens were herded into a smaller room where each signed a document in front of a judge, and was handed a most important and precious piece of paper, a Certificate of Citizenship. I am not certain, but I do believe that the judge gave me a pleasant smile, and thanked my mother for bringing me to the ceremony. Contrast is always good for clarification.

Chapter 4

Brooklyn

There was another small pick-up truck or van involved in my mother's and my move from Manhattan to Brooklyn, and one of the first items to be unloaded was a tricycle she had obtained for me. The minute the tricycle hit the concrete sidewalk of the housing projects where we were to reside, I got on that bike and road it on the grounds of this public dwelling community for at least two hours. I had never been afforded such space and relative safety ever in my life thus far. There were also grassy areas bordering the concrete walkways which I had now made a *tricycleway* on this sunny afternoon. I was so happy! We had been assigned Apartment 6D in this six-story building surrounded by both taller and shorter buildings in the complex. The apartment contained one bedroom, one living room, one kitchen, and—most importantly—one bathroom which only the two of us utilized. My mother slept in the bedroom, and I slept on the couch in the living room. The living room served several purposes, including a playroom and a schoolwork room. My social media was an Emerson radio on which I listened to WCBS or WOR programs mostly on Sundays, and best of all Martin Block's "Make Believe Ballroom" on

Saturday morning on which the top hits were counted down.

Saturday morning was also filled with assigned nonnegotiable chores. Cleaning the living room and bathroom (broom and mop and rag—no vacuum); taking the clothes (yes, sorted first) to the laundry room, where one waited for a washer to become vacant, and then for a device called an *extractor*, and then for an actual working dryer. The clothes were rolled to and from the laundry room in a shopping cart in need of new wheels. Needless to say, I did not always hear all of my Saturday radio show. Of course, the living room and bathroom had to pass inspection before I could proceed to the next event. Any shortcuts in the domestic process were met with swift verbal correction, and then physical adjustments. The goal was to be able to complete all chores by noon, have lunch, and go outside to play punchball or stickball or hide-and-seek or skelly or hopscotch or even jump rope. There were no gender-specific games, although the girls rarely played ball with the boys. Some eventually played with the boys'. . ., well, never mind!

The community was ethnically and racially mixed. Next door to me in 6E, a three-bedroom apartment, was an Irish family with two parents and six children. On the fourth floor in an adjacent building was a German family with two parents and three boys. Several buildings away was a Jewish family with five boys and two parents. I mention the Jewish family because I was very friendly with one of the boys and studied Hebrew with him in preparation for his Bar Mitzvah. In fact, I learned Hebrew so well that his mother stated that the ceremony should be held for me rather than him. The actual event was quite something, I recall. Yes, I was the only Black person in attendance. The City Housing Authority Property (*the projects*) actually consumed two very large square blocks. To the north was a predominantly Irish community of single-family homes; to the south, an exclusively Italian community of single-family homes with the exception of one street. The projects were considered dangerous by the residents of both these communities, and, ironically, the Irish dare not venture into the Italian neighborhood, and vice versa. For reasons which shall soon be revealed, I was able to traverse with relative ease in all three communities, although I must admit that real danger did lurk around most corners of the buildings in my project community.

I spent grades three through eight as a student in St. Agnes Parochial School, where I was the top academic student each year but rarely recognized for that achievement until eighth grade so as not to annoy the parents of the Irish and Italian pupils who had to cope with my being there in the first place. There were two groups at each grade level with about 60 pupils in each class, about two or three of us Negroes in each. Everyone peacefully coexisted, as I recall, and the White girls particularly liked me. I was smart, polite, and careful. We were instructed by the Sisters of St. Joseph, overseen by a very Irish Pastor who really enjoyed beer and wine, at least judging from his breath. The school was located on that one street in the Italian section which housed a few Irish families; the church was a cathedral-like structure located one block from the school. Every Monday, we were marched over to the church to rehearse hymns for the following Sunday (made no sense to me—a Friday would have been more appropriate) and to attend Benediction. Benediction was a ritual involving incense and a gold fixture called a Monstrance. No more need be said.

Allow me to fast-forward to seventh grade, in which I decided it would be neat to become an altar boy. The altar boy assisted the priest at Mass and wore a black cassock and white surplice, or a long black dress-like garment, and a white smock-like thingy. The only requirement as explained to me was to memorize the Latin responses and know when to bow, genuflect, kneel, and stand. How hard could that be for someone who had mastered fractions in the second semester of fifth grade after only a few classes with Sister Mary R (nicknamed Reggie Van Gleason III after a popular television character of the time)!)? Being the outspoken and popular seventh grader that I was, I proudly announced to my classmates that I was going to study the Latin needed to become an altar boy. I was told by one of my male classmates that such could not ever occur because I was colored. Citizenship Day immediately crossed through my mind, and thus I was incentivized not only to learn the Latin but also to be the best at it. I did and I was. During the eighth grade, I was called out of class to serve as an altar boy at several funeral masses, ofttimes for the deceased of prominent Italian families. Discretion prevents me from mentioning any surnames, but suffice to say I was tipped nicely by men in black suits with bulges in the shoulder area. Every once in a while, there was a wedding involving the families, and I was sought to assist at the nuptial Mass, which also resulted in monetary appreciation. One of the honors for the lead altar boy was to serve as master at Midnight Mass on Christmas, and in a similar role for the Easter Vigil. I accomplished both of those tasks as the first and only person of my race to do so.

Every summer, one of the kids from the projects died, and sometimes an adult. There were two causes of death of my playmates. One was being hit by a car while crossing the street to go to May's Candy Store; the other, from falling out of a window of one of the higher built (fourteen-story) buildings. On one of these occasions, the authorities did not arrive for a good hour after the fall, and we all stared at the body covered in a white sheet laying on the grass. There were also police car chases with gunfire as one would see in the movies, but we had the good sense to hit the ground to avoid the bullets. One of the automobile/child tragedies resulted in the mother of the victim running to the scene in her housecoat wielding a large knife from her kitchen. The police on the scene prevented any additional deaths. We all knew that one of us was not going to make it to the reopening of school; we just never knew which one of us, and took every precaution not to be a victim. You might be wondering about gangs. Yes, there were those, but they operated independent of our childhood playing companions and acquaintances. You may recall those funerals of which I spoke earlier. Running extremely close to our overall community was a waterway called the Gowanus Canal, into which all types of debris were thrown, and upon which sailed barges bringing goods (coal, mostly) from who knows where. With some regularity, a body was fished out of said canal by the police, usually a person who may have erred somehow in the performance of his work duties. We shall leave it there!

Eighth grade was absolutely terrific! There was Arlene, Felicia, Georgette, and other females whose gradual enlargements I observed during our time together since third grade. The syllabus was inadequate for my academic needs and skills, so I spent the afternoons of the second semester of eighth grade as an office assistant to the Principal, Sister A. Actually, I ran the office every afternoon, my first taste of school administration and leadership. One of my jobs was balancing the books for the candy money. Candy was sold to the students in all grades each and every day after lunch (cost: 1 cent each—120 to a box). I got to see the actual invoicing. What a markup! What a profit! Such capitalism within Catholicism! Terrific lessons at 12 years of age!

Other than girls and money, there was also politics—what a triad for a Black eighth grader in Irish/Italian Brooklyn. I had been elected president of the class in September of 1956, a role which yielded some notoriety and access. Practicing how to use such power was fun and, of course, beneficial to my future and my career. There came a point in time in late spring when one of the girls wore a "see-thru" blouse to school. The uniforms were, of course, modest for the Catholic young ladies so as not to arouse, I guess, the good Catholic young men. This particular day, however, PF wore her sheer blouse, and wore it well. How enjoyable for us boys, until such time—and it was not long into the school day—that Sister Principal sent her home to change into a more Catholic-school garment. We were devastated and my classmates called upon the president to intervene or at least gain an explanation. So off I went to Sister Principal to make inquiry as to the reason for PF's temporary dismissal from our sight. Sister Principal leaned back in her chair, looked me dead in the eye, and said, "Peter, you know why I sent her home." So much for the power of the presidency!

The top two events of eighth grade were attending, via subway in Manhattan, the Cecil B. DeMille film, *The Ten Commandments*, with the entire class, and then, in a small group, wending our way to Queens to see the Pope in his motorcade. It was not the Pope (I believe it was Pius XII,) that made it so exciting; it was the adventure of about five of us travelling away from the neighborhood on a school day. It was legal. The diocese had closed all the schools for the day due to the Pope's visit. It was so much fun figuring out which trains to take in order to get to Queens, where the Pope's motorcade was scheduled to travel. There were five of us—three White girls, a White boy, and yours truly, all of us at the top academic level of the class. We got to Queens without incident (yes, a few looks here and there) and even climbed over a fence to gain a

good view of His Holiness. Imagine that—
Charlton Heston and a Pope were the highlights
of my life that year! I speak with forked tongue as
Tonto, the Lone Ranger's Indian companion,
might say.

The true highlight of eighth grade was
being awarded a full four-year scholarship to
Regis High School, a Jesuit secondary school
located in Manhattan to educate the top male
academic students of the New York metropolitan
area. St. Agnes had been awarded three slots for
its top eighth graders to take the entrance exam,
and I was one of the three who filled those slots,
along with an Irish kid and an Italian kid. Two of
the three of us were successful in our quest. On
the day of the exam, my mother, the Irish kid, and
I journeyed via subway to East 84th Street, where
the exam was administered. The other student
opted for other transport. While the 2,000 or so
eighth graders were taking the exam, my mother
spent the three hours in St. Ignatius Loyola
Church on Park Avenue, across from the school,
praying for the success of the St. Agnes boys. The
entrance examination was difficult, as it sought to
determine the extent of the students' verbal, math,
and reasoning skills. The phrase *to separate the
men from the boys* was certainly applicable in
terms of the depth of the entrance exam.

It was a bigger deal than I had thought (actually, I had never heard of Regis High School until I was told I was taking this exam) because Sister Principal paraded the two of us around the school to each and every classroom, where we received applause, prompted of course by the principal. It was a first for St. Agnes, and quite possibly a last with respect to entering freshmen at Regis, and certainly a first for a Negro student.

Chapter 5

Regis High School and My Mother

This is indeed a strange juxtaposition of influences, but there are parallels and reasons, one of which involves the reality that the marvelous Miss Carter would be with us for only eight more years: the four years of my high school sojourn and the four years of college. So, as we come to a midpoint of my formal education, we shall also focus on half of the reason for my success—the other half being a congregation of priests and brothers known as the Society of Jesus, or the Jesuits. It is the spring of 1957, and I am sitting in the Office of the Headmaster of Regis High with my mother, and another entering freshman and his father. It was the custom for the headmaster to personally interview each entering freshman and his parent(s). I do not recall any of my mother's questions, but I do too well recall the question from CS's father. He inquired to Father Headmaster as to why the boys had to receive three years of instruction in Ancient Greek. The Jesuit priest leaned back in his chair and said, "That's the way we do it." So ended the Q and A. I do recall the unspoken word of maternal approval for that response which said, "This is where I want my son to be educated," and educated I was.

From age 3 through 13, not too many specifics come to mind with respect to my mother. She was more of a strong silent soul. There was the time when I was really frustrated with all of my Saturday chores as a young boy, and asked for a sister who could do this work. What followed was a very long and serious lecture with respect to the role of women in the world, and sweeping, washing, and other purely domestic duties were not the reasons they were placed on earth. I have never forgotten the core of that lecture, and certainly have operated accordingly. I certainly never asked for a sister again, nor did I ever view women as anything other than equal to (perhaps even better than) men. She was quite sickly and hence did not and could not really work outside of the home. I came to know that we received public financial assistance, known as welfare, said checks arriving on the 1st and 15th of every month. She could certainly make a little go a very long way, and kept me from knowing how poor we really were.

Either through intelligence or stupidity, I spoke out quite a bit, or out of turn, as my mother would describe it. The penalty for such verbiage was a swift blow to the mouth, usually resulting in a tooth piercing the lip, causing blood and a swelling. Due to my own behavior, there were many times when ice wrapped in a washcloth had to be applied to my lip. She also did not tolerate untruths or what she determined to be rude or disrespectful behavior. The penalty for such infractions was what both she and I called *a beating*. The object for the administration of this corporal punishment was a leather strap that she somehow always had handy. On those occasions when she could not readily locate the strap, she made me remove my own belt. The irony here is that in either case, she was sure to expose my bottom in order to administer the stinging blows. She truly believed that since she bore me, she could also un-bear me, if you get my drift. By the way, better her strap than a policeman's nightstick or firearm. However, when I had my tonsils and adenoids surgically removed, a kinder and gentler person could not be found.

You may have noticed my referring to her as *Miss Carter*. Well, that is correct, and it was not until years into my adulthood that I realized that my mother and biological father were never married. I would occasionally ask about my father as I was growing up, and was told that he had died and that his name was Joseph. How fitting! How clever! How poignant! She had told me that she asked God for a son, and that He had given her one. Her mother, the aforementioned and described Grandma, had a different surname altogether which was never explained. When Miss Carter's stay at her mother's Harlem apartment ended, I recall (as a five-year-old) hearing said, "You and your little bastard can get the hell out of here." Twenty years later, those words made sense.

My mother insisted on taking me places. How she managed to do these things, I never knew. She took me to the Ringling Bros. and Barnum & Bailey Circus, the Rodeo (starring Roy Rogers and Dale Evans), the Central Park Zoo, the Bronx Zoo, Central Park itself, Prospect Park, and Coney Island, as well as to meet Hopalong Cassidy, a renowned radio/television cowboy. Of special note was the Macy's Thanksgiving Day Parade, which we attended several times as well as the Christmas Spectacular at Radio City Music Hall. The parade was only a subway ride (10 cents for her; free for me) as was the trip to see the Radio City Rockettes, which only cost 95 cents plus we got to see a full-length movie, too. The Macy's parade was usually followed by a trip to St. Francis of Assisi Church on 32nd Street. One year, she took ill at the church, actually fainted, and was transported by ambulance to St. Vincent's Hospital. I may have been 9 years old at the time, receiving a ride in an ambulance from 32nd Street to 11th Street on Thanksgiving Day.

For a woman with health issues, she was tough, and instilled in me to be tough and not take *no* for an answer (except, of course, from her). At the parades, she made get up to the front row at the police line and sit there with the White kids and get a good full view. She insisted that I be polite, but not be a pushover. Even though the world had not been kind to her, she urged me to be kind and caring of other living things. She thought a pet or two may be appropriate for her only child, and so at various intervals in my youth, I had goldfish, at least two turtles, a cat, and even a small chick. She demanded excellence, frequently asking why I got only a 94 on any given math test in sixth grade and not a 100. She eased off a bit in high school, realizing how difficult Regis was in comparison with St. Agnes or St. Catherine of Genoa, even though she always wanted me to be an honor-roll student, and not merely on the list of merit. I made the honor roll once in my four years, just for her.

So let us examine my four years at a special high school located on East 84th Street in Manhattan between Park and Madison Avenues. Tall apartment buildings in this area were the norm, and each had a doorman. This was a far cry from the low-income housing projects of Brooklyn to which I had become accustomed. Each day, I walked to the Bergen Street Station, took the D train one stop to Borough Hall, changed for the A train, went to Broadway Nassau, and changed there for the Lexington Avenue going uptown to 86th Street. Such was the reverse when I left school each day at about 4:30 pm as I enjoyed being in that environment and had a number of afterschool activities. Like my mother, precision was demanded, and rules were meticulously enforced. And like my mother, too, caring abounded.

To continue this literary marriage of my mother and my high school, I am forced to temporarily jump ahead to my senior year, when this strong woman of color took on the Jesuit establishment and negotiated a full four-year college scholarship, inclusive of tuition, fees, books, and an on-campus job for her son. Her conversation started with the Regis guidance counselor, and ended with the Vice President of Fordham University. I have no idea as to the contents of any of these conversations, only that Miss Carter was live and in person for all of them. The Fordham chapters shall follow, I assure you, but for now, we return to Regis.

Regis admitted 210 freshmen in September of 1957, and graduated 157 seniors in June of 1961. This was one tough academic place, and keep in mind it only admitted the cream of the crop of Catholic eighth-grade boys. At the end of each semester, those who had not met the standard, a passing (75 or better) grade in all subjects, were dismissed from the school. To make matters even more stressful, a student who "failed" a subject for a semester had to attain a grade of 80 or better in all subjects in the following semester, or face the educational gallows. One of the first victims of the system was a rich White kid from Long Island who finished his freshman year in a Nassau County Catholic high school, where he went on to be the valedictorian three-and-a-half years later. So, what were these subjects which so challenged us students, and caused possible annihilation at the end of a semester? Latin, Greek, French, or German, Mathematics, Science, Social Studies, and Religion. There is no need to get into the specifics or reasons we studied all these subjects. Suffice to say, by the way, there were no electives, no choices.

I bet you are wondering about the racial composition of this secondary school I attended. Well, of that 210, eventually 157, there was one of me. I was a pretty big deal, being the student manager of the bookstore, the head manager of the basketball team, a senior usher at Friday Mass (oh, yes, we went to Mass every Friday at 11:15 am), an actor in two plays, and treasurer of various dance committees. There was no doubt in my mind that I was the first Negro to be in such leadership roles at the school. I had keys to all sorts of storerooms and offices, and even the most enviable of them all—the elevator.

For many of my classmates, I was also the first and only colored person they had ever seen up close and personal. Most overcame that trauma. Some did not, and expressed some disparaging remarks both in and out of my presence. I was never elected to any school office by my peers, for example, although I did meet my two best and dearest friends at Regis. One of them(JC) and I ate lunch every day for our four years at the school, and shared a ride to the prom. The other(TW) was the best man at my first wedding. We met on the D train as were subwaying to school as freshmen. I learned to survive the slings and arrows of stares, looks, comments, party invitations not received, and doors not held. There were some faculty members who were clearly bigoted and prejudiced, and showed favor to the majority students. But then there was the Assistant Principal (co-titled the prefect of discipline), one of the more precious of the Earth's human beings and a Jesuit. He was firm, fair, and good at his job. We feared him in a loving sort of way. He eventually left the priesthood, and according to informed sources, fathered six children with a Native American woman in the Northwestern part of these United States. I learned, too, to appreciate the kind thoughts and good wishes which emanated from the cafeteria tables and classrooms and corridors, while ignoring the negative from the ignorant. The majority of the people with whom I came in contact were tolerant of my Blackness with little resentment for the heights to which I had risen. I took on extracurricular student responsibilities because my mother always told me to do what I wanted to do, despite any seeming obstacles. "No human being is better than you are, Peter," were her frequent words.

As manager of the varsity basketball team, I had to attend all the games, both "home" and "away," some of which were at night. Walking home from the subway station at night in my neighborhood was an "iffy" situation at best, and a dangerous feat at worst, especially for a teenaged Black male. The walk was about three city blocks from Smith and Warren Streets to Bond and Baltic Streets. There was one occasion when I was returning home from a game, almost at the end of my walk, when I heard some rustling in the bushes, voices, and then about four individuals around me. Two of the four had drawn their guns, while one of them spoke, saying, "Where are you going, boy?" No member of this group of White men had identified himself in any way. As it turned out, they were all police detectives during what I guess a monthly cleansing of the neighborhood, making any Black male a target. What had caused their ire was that I hastened my pace once I had heard the footsteps getting closer to me. Fortunately, my ability to articulate enabled me to clearly explain that I was walking home, having attended a night basketball game at my Manhattan Catholic high school. Three of the four cops accompanied me to the front door of my building, which was a mere five minutes from this police "stop." To fully express how afraid I was during this ordeal would involve descriptors inappropriate for this piece of literature. I almost died that night at the hands or the weapons of New York's Finest. I had survived both TB and the NYPD prior to the age of 17.

Chapter 6

CYO Day Camp, Coney Island, Brooklyn

During the summers from the beginning of high school through college and into the beginning of my career, I was an employee at a place called CYO Day Camp. CYO were the initials for the Catholic Youth Organization, a subsidiary of Catholic Charities, a religious welfare entity to assist people in need in a myriad of ways. The CYO wing sponsored several programs, among which were summer programs for children in several locations. The pastor of St. Agnes Parish was a friend of the priest who headed the CYO, and referred me for a summer job as a junior counselor. It was the summer between my freshman and sophomore years at Regis, and unknown to me, I was to spend ten summers at this place, located on one city square block on Surf Avenue in the Coney Island section of Brooklyn.

CYO Day Camp became my life's best experience where I learned how to truly understand White people, and thus be very successful in telling them what to do. It was only three summers at the camp until I was given a supervisory role by the camp director, a young Irishman (who appeared much older to me than he actually was) with a very right-wing conservative bent. He was a social worker by degree and this was his actual job with

Catholic Charities. My later analysis was that he had been given this summer leadership gig as an "extra" thus saving the parent organization quite a bit of money. He, although nowhere near a liberal or promoter of minorities, decided that this black teenager was to be a rising star in his organization. At 17 or 18 years of age, I was in charge of the transportation for the 2,000 campers who travelled to the property daily from every parish in Brooklyn in about 20 school buses. I was also the office lead as well as the equipment manager, and at times prepared payroll. It was here at CYO Day Camp where I learned the administrative skills which were to be the basis of my future successes. Mr. R, as he was called, was an amazing and difficult boss. He both expected and demanded perfection. There was never room for an error, a mistake, a human foible, and God forbid one ever offered an excuse for a faux pas. He was stern, his voice was powerful and loud, and one was never at a loss with regard to his displeasure with regard to your performance in any particular task. He instilled fear in most, respect in some, and admiration in a few. I admired, respected, and feared him, but most of all loved him like the father I never had. He made me who I was to become, and I have been forever grateful. In order to squeeze every possible use out of the Surf Avenue property as possible, after day camp hours and on weekends, there was a phenomenon known as the Surf Club, where 110 Irish and Italian families enjoyed the pool and their own cooking on their own grills. Yes, you guessed correctly—this black person also had an administrative role with regard to these White families who were members of the Surf Club.

So here I was surrounded by people most of whom had no association with colored, Negro, African American, or Black people other than at Surf Avenue. This fact was also true of the counselors who worked at camp daily. Being Black in this world of Whites during the summer and during the school year was truly an eye-opener. So many of my CYO associates have become lifelong friends (from adolescence to Social Security) as we grew up together from different worlds that maybe were not that different. We just looked different. We learned that we shared similar joys and sorrows and disappointments. Similar matters made us glad; similar matters made us sad. Certainly, there were bigots in this group of teen counselors and adult club members, but they carefully concealed their true feelings to the best of their abilities. I suspect it is quite difficult for a White person to interact with a Black person and consider him or her to be an actual equal peer, especially if such interaction is not an ordinary occurrence. CYO afforded us all the opportunity to grow together and know together. It provided a platform for me to show that a black boy/man can be a friend, a coworker, a boss.

The campers (six to fourteen years old) were divided by age and gender, with Native American names assigned to the boys' groups and bird names to the girls' groups. The oldest girls' group (thirteen and fourteen years old) was aptly named the Hawks. The children looked like their counselors in this 98% White environment. The youngest boys (six years old) were the Sioux and their girl counterparts the Jays. The oldest boys (fourteen years old) proudly had the title of Iroquois. We took the children on various field trips, including the Coca Cola Bottling Company, where each person received a free Coke at the end of the tour. There was a thing called "Bus Park" which merely indicated the mode of transportation to a park to play softball. The program was rounded out with arts and crafts and music and dance, and cartoons on rainy days.

The groups ran about 30 boys or girls each with a senior counselor (seventeen or eighteen years old) and one or two junior counselors (fourteen, fifteen, and sixteen years old) at the helm. Campers' parents packed the children's lunches daily, which were collected and then refrigerated by group until the noon hour. My first senior counselor was named Mike; my first junior counselor was Steve. Also populating this very special place were Jane and Joan and Maria and Lenny and Carl and Andy and Al and Gene and Joe and Peggy and Diane and Mary Ellen. These were all teenagers from very basic white households whose mothers were housewives and fathers were firemen, policemen, and sanitation workers. Some of these counselors from 1960 remain friends and associates today, sixty years later, in 2020. "Surf Avenue, Coney Island, Brooklyn, New York, USA . . . We travelled there in the buses, in the buses every day…" were the words in a song written for a camp musical. Mr. R believed in bringing a well-rounded program to the young boys and girls of Brooklyn who spent their summer at the camp in three two-week sessions and one three-week session. Among those boys and girls was even the son of a famous professional baseball player (Brooklyn Dodgers, first base) whose father would occasionally stop by to pick him up. What a thrill that was!

This was a very special place, and even though I was not part of the eventual nuptial statistics for obvious reasons, I had warm feelings for my camp family members, and they for me and for one another. It is impossible to put into words what happened on that square block eight hours every day, or five hours every evening, or twelve hours every Saturday and Sunday. So let us just call it our own magical kingdom, without the cost of admission and waiting in long lines. Oh my, I forgot to mention that a mere ten blocks away was New York City's largest and greatest amusement park named for the community which housed it: Coney Island. However, we did not need the rides and cotton candy to sustain the happiness which seemed to permeate the camp. Well, maybe Nathan's (maker of the just the best hot dogs) and the Cyclone (a roller coaster with lots of twists and turns) may be the exceptions with regard to a complement to our own Disneyland at Surf Avenue between West 27th and West 28th Streets.

Chapter 7

The Bronx and Fordham University

You recall that I mentioned my mother's high-powered negotiations to afford me a free education at one of the nation's best institutions of higher learning. For whatever the reason, room and board were not included in the deal, so once again we moved—this time from Brooklyn to The Bronx, that borough just north of Manhattan, which contains a definite article in its name. The Bronx, like ancient Gaul, was divided into at least three parts. The part which we could afford was called the East Bronx (maybe the South Bronx), where the predominant language was Puerto Rican Spanish. My mother obtained an apartment with two bedrooms, a kitchen, and a bath on Stebbins Avenue, adjacent to East 163rd Street, walking and hearing distance from an elevated interborough subway station. Also within walking distance was a bus stop where a public vehicle took me to college in about twenty minutes' time.

The College of Arts and Sciences of Fordham University, housed on the Rose Hill Campus (Fordham Road, 190th Street), was populated by 2,000 undergraduate males, of which seven were not of the Caucasian persuasion. The majority of the majority had very little experience with human beings who did not share their whiteness. We blacks were looked upon and admired for our seeming athletic prowess, and nothing more. Not to destroy the myth, there was to be a basketball All-American in this gang of seven, and to totally shatter all beliefs and expectations, a Rhodes scholar, a criminal judge, an author, a university professor, a law enforcement professional, and a public school administrator.

The campus was huge and well landscaped. My classes were spread out among at least four different buildings and the campus center. My major: Classical Languages (Latin and Greek)! Why not, given the high school I had attended? My activities: campus politician! Why not, again? I was popular, and could garner a large number of votes from those boys who had entered with me from schools similar to mine. You did notice I said *boys*. There were no female students at Fordham College in the early 1960s, and had not been since the school's founding in 1841. I suspect there had not been many, if any, African American students either. So here I was, a black kid on the ballot for Freshman Class office running for Vice President—definitely a first. And this black kid and his running mates won! In my second year, I had the audacity to run for Treasurer, and that ticket won also. This was way too much for the student body to absorb, as we shall read soon.

The accomplishments of my years as a campus politician were significant, filling the treasury with thousands of dollars through the promotion of musical concerts on campus starring some very notable acts from that era. In my junior year, I took a rest from active politics and became the sports director of the college radio station, WFUV-FM. I provided the play-by-play for the basketball games as well as a few crew races, and far too many home baseball games. I also kept my finger in the bowl of concert promotions. Although success had been our hallmark, one particular event did not do so well. We booked one of the top black recording artists of the time, Ray Charles, and lost our shirts. Fordham was not ready for that in 1963. Fortunately, the Kingston Trio; Peter, Paul and Mary; the Clancy Brothers, and even the Dave Brubeck Quartet drew "sold-out" crowds, enhancing the reputation of the Fordham College Concert Committee which I co-chaired. There was a group gaining popularity in Liverpool, England, at the time named the Beatles. Yours truly had been given an inside line on this quartet of young musicians, and the opportunity to fly them into America and to Fordham for a debut concert. I turned down the opportunity, claiming that a group with such a name could never make it in the music world or in show business. This error in judgement and perception was and remains as the biggest mistake of my life.

In November of my junior year, I was on the second floor of the campus center for whatever the reason when the center's director, one of the few female administrators at Fordham, came running from her office. She was a formidable human being, devoid of any emotion we could discern, and we student leaders had to deal with her on a regular basis. No event could occur in the campus center without her approval. For example, during my four years, we arranged for a national television show whose focus was on folk music to tape a sixty-minute program in the campus center. We had to persuade Miss F, the director, that she should allow such a thing. Nothing could occur in that building, which had numerous meeting rooms, without the approval of this director. For the record, the phrase "Are you kidding me?" or just plain "No" did not present a problem for the vocabulary of this administrator. We (I) tread very carefully when approaching this woman for the use of a conference room or the ballroom or even the bathrooms. So, you could imagine our shock when we saw her come out of her office with tears in her eyes to announce that the president of the United States had been shot in Dallas, Texas.

As senior year approached, I took it upon myself to attempt the impossible: a run for student body president. There were some hurdles to be jumped prior to that feat, one of which was an appointment to a "Student Senate" seat in my junior year, a kind of political prerequisite. To ensure such did not happen, the majority saw to it that I lost by one vote by waking a member of the council who was quite ill, and almost carrying him to the campus center, where the vote was being taken. Several months thereafter, I waged a vigorous campaign for the top office, and when it appeared that there was a possibility for this historic first for an African American student, the student press and other forces persuaded the student body at large that Fordham just could not have a Black student body president. And such was to be the case, not a first here. Other than race, there was a real platform issue: the return of football as a varsity sport to Fordham Rose Hill. My opponent, who also happened to be a proponent of right-wing views on the national scene, was in favor of the return of football, and I (the Beatles naysayer) was opposed to such a campaign issue, claiming it was an empty promise, impossible to be realized. I lost the election, but learned so much about being Black—the truth about being Black. Always tread carefully; you are not and shall never be one of THEM.

In the fall of 1964, football returned to Fordham with a sold-out crowd for an NYU-Fordham game. I was still the WFUV sports director and provided excellent radio coverage of the game, complete with sideline and post-game commentary. Elections have consequences! One of the positive results of this interaction with some extremely white people was a mutual respect which lasted well over fifty years. My right-wing opponent matured to become an active leader for the civil rights of the less connected, and his running mate a president of one the nation's leading academic universities. Our senior year was filled with local and national controversy, including a conflict in a place called Vietnam. There came a point in time when our speaker bureau invited the royal reigning head of that country and her daughter to campus. When the madame and her daughter walked onto the stage, we non-coeducational males broke out in tumultuous applause. We were not applauding the politics, but the exquisite beauty of the daughter. None of us, Black or White, had seen any female that beautiful. OK, we rarely saw young females, period! The television press, one network in particular (no, not *that* one—it had not been established yet), destroyed us on the Evening News that day, for which an apology by the network's renowned correspondent had to be rendered several days later.

In June of 1965, graduation day finally arrived. Four years of Latin, Greek, philosophy, and theology had ended. More importantly, my mother's prayer and wish to be alive for my college graduation was answered. In August of 1965, she was admitted to St. Vincent's Hospital in

Manhattan and died of cancer of the upper left bowel a few months later. The guest speaker at this Fordham graduation was the Vice President of the United States at the time. He spoke to us from a podium erected on the steps of the campus landmark building, Keating Hall. The imposing Keating Hall Tower with its four-faced clock was the backdrop for the Vice President; at the forefront, four imposing Secret Service agents stared us down during his entire speech. We really felt intimidated by these G-men with guns almost at the ready. What an experience! In retrospect, I suppose the White House had a vivid recollection of our reception for the daughter of the royal head of the country of Vietnam, with whom we were in full conflict by the time of my graduation.

Chapter 8

Job Hunting and My First Job

You may recall that in the package my mother had negotiated with the Jesuits was a provision for an on-campus job. That job was at the front desk of the university library. I was soon promoted to the reference desk, and then eventually to the number two position, which involved visiting other libraries and offices on campus as a courier and messenger, and—yes—a key. I certainly needed to work just to pay the bus fare to get to and from home and campus, not to mention lunch and personal items. And then there was dating! No, I have not mentioned that activity since my nursery school experience. Ah, that should be a separate chapter all together. Returning to the job thing, I also obtained a position in the Receiving Department of a major department store located on 33rd Street in Manhattan. The man who hired me was terrific and his successor even better. My job was on the 11th floor of the building, where the merchandise shipped to the store was opened and tagged with price labels. I worked there three nights a week and Saturdays during the latter years of college, taking the public rapid transit system from Fordham Road to Pennsylvania Station. I even worked there during my first years of my professional career. In fact, personnel leadership tried to recruit me to come with them full-time as part of a management training program upon my graduation from college. I declined the offer, which did pay more than my first job, by the way. During my senior year, I was promoted to supervise the night toy operation, which involved checking in and tagging the merchandise shipped to 32nd Street and elevated to the sixth floor. With a crew of five other males, I handled this assignment for about three Christmas seasons (October 1 to December 31), and loved it. I really liked the world of retail; it was exciting, especially during the holiday buying frenzy. The head of the toy department, the buyer, was a balding Irishman, similar in personality and demeanor to my boss at CYO. He left every day at 4:40 pm in order to catch his train to the suburbs, except on Thursdays, his "late night." I learned so much on Thursdays from Mr. MacD. I suspect that he was the person who recommended me to personnel for full-time employment, although he never revealed that. I later found out that he was one of the top five toy buyers in the United States.

This retail department store with nine selling floors each covering a city square block eventually went out of business as a national chain. So I had made the correct decision not to commit to a full-time position upon college graduation. The store was extremely interested in recruiting me since given its hundreds of employees, there may have been ten blacks, if that many, and only one in a management position (of sorts) as head of stock. Such made perfect sense because the majority of the Black people worked in the stockrooms. Even the toy department stock person was a black male of some years who saw me as some sort of a threat. He had a good reason for his concern. He was lazy; I was energetic. He may have had an eighth-grade education; I was a college graduate. I was 21; he was at least 61. He was still hardly working long after my employment had concluded. The store personnel executive made it quite clear to me that if I were to sign up with them that I would quickly become the first Black person in the history of the store to reach a top managerial position. So much for that "first"!

Before we leave this portion of my work experience as I entered my 20s, I must share a little tidbit about how my altar boy experience back at St. Agnes was very helpful during my department store days. While I was working in the receiving department, there came a point in time when I was asked to join the retail workers union. Due to the fact that my salary was meager, I did not need to have union dues deducted therefrom on a weekly basis. Upon knowledge of my refusal to join the union, I was summoned to the "office" of the head of the union. It was unclear as to the actual location of the union boss' "office," since it just seemed like a little room to me in a mezzanine close to the actual receiving area where trucks came, were unloaded, and left. During my five minutes with this 'gentleman' and his 'assistants' I shared with him my knowledge of similar figures from my youth in Brooklyn. Our 'conversation' concluded with my being absolved of the demand to join the union. Definitely a "first," I had spoken with others of my ilk who had met with this person on the topic of union affiliation; each had become a union member subsequent to the encounter.

In the spring of 1965, it was time to start my pursuit of gainful employment as a soon-to-be college graduate who had majored in classical languages (Latin and Greek). Fortunately, from the age of about 9, I always wanted to be a teacher. Thus, my job pursuits led in the direction of secondary institutions of learning. Since my undergraduate studies were strictly academic in nature, I never obtained a governmental certificate from the state or from the city to teach at any level. Thus, my career path led only to parochial or private schools, either elementary or secondary. Speaking of legal documents, at some point during the early 1960s, I obtained my own United States citizenship credentials, thankfully without the drama associated with my mother's swearing-in. I realized that I needed documentation prior to my job search and college graduation. This process gave me the opportunity to officially add *E* as my middle initial, thus making Peter E. Carter my full legal name. By the way, I could have given myself any name I desired during the citizenship/naturalization process. It is the only occasion, I believe, other than marriage (for a female) in which a person can change his or her name without a fee and a legal hassle. So I became Peter E. Carter, instead of Peter Carter. Imagine, though, if I had opted for Mayer Goldstein or something. Neither name is very black, a fact which led to some interesting face-to-face surprises for potential employers and potential landlords. Not only is my name not very Black, but also my vocal expressions are not very Black because I never totally lost my British West Indian accent. I just melded and blended in a little Brooklynese with it, which resulted in fun and foul situations and confrontations, many of which were "firsts" especially for the ignorant white persons involved.

So, the pursuit for the beginning of a teaching career began with a few telephone calls, and letters of application. There were several places I knew were off-limits for me to seek, and I let discretion be the better part of valor. My brief resume, of course, showed my educational background as Regis and Fordham, so with a name like Carter, there was no hint as to my ethnicity. On two interview encounters, the representative for my potential future employer gasped upon the realization that Peter Carter, or even Peter E. Carter, was Black; after all, my paperwork did not connote same, and neither did the telephone conversation setting up the visit. Believe it or not, I enjoyed these encounters, and the manner in which the racist organizations of teaching and learning attempted to wiggle out of their uncomfortable situations. Two institutions, however, did respond in the affirmative with actual job offers. One was St. Peter's Preparatory School in Jersey City, New Jersey, operated by the Jesuits; the other was Nazareth High School in Brooklyn, New York, run by the Xaverian Brothers. For the $200 more a year offered at Nazareth, I accepted the position offered to me by another outstanding human being, the Principal, Brother T. This was indeed a strong and a brave individual, hiring a young black man to teach Latin and English at a Brooklyn diocesan high school serving the Irish and Italian male teenagers of the Flatbush, Rockaway, and Sheepshead Bay sections of the borough. I found out in time that there were a few existing faculty members opposed to my hiring once they learned that I was black. The students were not at all perturbed; actually, they perceived this as exciting—a true first for all of them.

Before we get into the nuts and bolts of my first teaching job, let me deal with, yes, you guessed it—my mother. There had been a third employment offer on the table, namely, a position with a professional promoter of concerts in the city and other major venues in these United States. RD and I had met while I was in college, and had done some work together. He, in fact, was the originator (in the 1960s) of summer concerts in Central Park. There was no way in Heaven or Hell I could tell my mother, who wanted me to be a doctor or lawyer, that I was going off to who knows where in the country to hang out with celebrities who sang, danced, and smoked whatever. It was hard enough for her to accept that I was going to become a teacher, which she considered "woman's work," even though she had dealt with male educational clerics during my Regis and Fordham days. I found that sexist point of view quite strange for a woman way ahead of her time when it came to female liberation issues. So teaching in Brooklyn it was, and a move back to that borough was next. She and I found a lovely two-bedroom apartment on Hawthorne Street in Flatbush, and moved there in August or so of 1965. She was admitted into the hospital shortly thereafter, and God took her back in October. She never benefitted from the fruits of any of my first paychecks from Nazareth High School. I was 21 years old.

To get to work involved a subway ride, and then a bus ride at the beginning until a colleague, another first-year teacher who lived near the subway and bus stops, offered to drive me to work. I met him at his home (actually, his parents' home) every morning. I was on my own for the return trip. My first day of teaching was memorable. I had two classes of First-Year Latin, one class of Second-Year Latin, one class of Second-Year English, one class of Fourth-Year English, and a study period. At the end of my first day, I came home, lay across my bed, and fell asleep for four hours. With the exception of crashing at home immediately after work, the rest of the school year was well spent in the instruction of these five classes of Brooklyn boys, visiting my mother in the hospital while she was still with us, and—wait for it—working at that aforementioned Manhattan retail department store during the holiday shopping season. Marking test papers on the subway became a very natural phenomenon, as had been studying Homer's *Odyssey* on a similar conveyance back in my high school years.

At Nazareth High School, I met men, PH especially, and boys (JW, JT, and EB) who would become lifelong friends. There were the monthly poker games, coffee in a diner close to the school after school dances which we chaperoned, a funeral, a wedding, a birth, and apartment hunting again. Teaching was all that I had expected and more. The ability and the responsibility for sharing information with youth of which they had no prior knowledge was awesome. Each day, each class, was a new and exciting experience, an educational experience which carried forth for forty years. The students learned from me, and I learned from them as well as from my teaching colleagues, very bright men of the Caucasian persuasion. One of my early lessons in the education profession was that of labor negotiations with management, and the strategies which were inherent in the success of said activities for both parties. The greatest lesson, however, was the importance of instilling in one's students the sense of caring about not only their acquisition of the "ablative absolute" but also, more importantly, their appreciation for knowledge, fact, truth, and themselves.

My first teaching job was very special because the school was a very special place, not unlike CYO Day Camp. The bonds which were built among colleagues and students here were unique. The majority of the white folks here accepted one another as people, not as part of any particular group or ethnicity or race. We were all just educators. One of my extra-curricular assignments was as the coach of the speech and debate team. The school had been in existence for only a few years, so there was no win/loss record for any of the competitive activities (with the exception of track). I had fun and success with the team, even defeating at one round of a tournament the top team of the region and the state. That all-girls' team, by the way, was coached by a fellow Fordham grad who went on to eventually become the president of New York University. That sole victory was so sweet for so many reasons. I also coached the junior varsity basketball team for two games during the regular coach's illness. We were victorious for both games, making me, in good humor of course, an undefeated high school basketball coach. These were all "firsts" for this young Black teacher.

Chapter 9

The Funeral, the Wedding, and the Birth

Clearly missing from my narrative thus far, as previously noted, is interaction with the opposite sex (same sex was out of the question in my environment of the '50s, '60s, and '70s). In our senior year at Fordham, the Jesuits decided that female students might not be a bad idea, so they found two hundred of the brightest and most Catholic 18-year-old girls in the countryside and enrolled them in a school called Thomas More College. Of the two hundred, two were black (light skinned, but black nonetheless). I dated both of them—no, not at the same time, but almost! One young lady oddly enough lived directly across the street from me in the Bronx on Stebbins Avenue. Her desire was to become a medical doctor. The other young lady lived in Westchester County (Pearl River, I believe) and was already the mother of a two-year old boy. My mother disliked her instinctively, claiming that she had too much experience for me. Details are not necessary, but she was a lot more fun than the pre-med lady. Unfortunately, since we had this parent/girlfriend issue which truly manifested itself at my graduation, the relationship was doomed for cessation.

There came a point in time when one of the other six Black college classmates introduced me to a lady from Brooklyn, a graduate from a three-year commercial high school, an employee of the New York Telephone Company (now Verizon), and the eldest of four girls. She and her family resided in a building in the Williamsburg section of Brooklyn, said building constructed to be a store on the main floor, and living quarters on each of the two floors above. Her visit to my mother in the hospital rendered an approval for marriage as best as a mother could under a cancerous condition. The viewing and the funeral were attended by all sorts of people, including college professors, my eighth-grade lay teacher, some high school teachers, including the headmaster, fellow Nazareth teachers, and students. Of particular note on the roster of attendees was my grandmother—remember her? She was full of criticisms with regard to the attire I had selected for her daughter to lie in state, namely, a business suit which I found quite appropriate for a myriad of reasons. My mother was buried in a dress instead. So much for (grand)son power! There were no insurance dollars for the costs of the viewing and funeral, but somehow there was a tie-in from the funeral home management to CYO Day Camp clergy, and the invoice was voided. I suspect this was truly a first for all concerned; I was never given the details.

In August of 1966, I was married to Laura, the lady from Williamsburg, by my College Dean, my High School Principal, my Nazareth Student Advisor, and a Protestant Minister at St. Ignatius of Loyola Church (not the Park and 84th Street structure) on Rogers Avenue in Brooklyn. All the bridesmaids were Black; all the groomsmen were White. We honeymooned in Montego Bay, Jamaica, and she gave birth to my beautiful daughter, Elizabeth Ann, in early May. As Laura's contractions occurred at more regular intervals, I knew it was time for us to be leaving for the hospital. The hospital was located north of our Hawthorne Street home, and taxi drivers were afraid of taking fares in that direction. I had to actually beg and then pre-pay a taxi driver to take us to the hospital. We made it with some (but not much) time to spare on May 6, 1967. I had never begged for anything in my life up until then, and never begged for anything again. I took driving lessons, and bought a Mercury Comet from my dear friend and teaching colleague.

Chapter 10

Moving in and Moving on, and Another Birth

We knew that our now family would very quickly outgrow the current dwelling, so the search for another apartment was necessary. What we did not know was that the bigotry and racism that faced us with regard to transportation to a maternity ward would also face us in procuring suitable and favorable living quarters in most parts of Brooklyn. I recall one day having seen an ad for an apartment, calling the number advertised, and driving over to see the place during my "prep" period. When I arrived fifteen minutes after my call, I was informed by the agent that the apartment had just been rented. When I returned, I told my white students, many of whom had attended Elizabeth's baptismal celebration. They were not pleased with the reality of Mr. Carter's world, and very surprised that their teacher was denied a place to live for himself and his family. This rejection occurred on two other occasions in a week's time. A corporate enterprise and builder of apartment complexes had advertised widely in the press listing available locations. I went to the main office and was given a list of places to visit. My dear friend and white teaching colleague arrived at the same office and was given a list with entirely different addresses. We switched lists. The various onsite building managers were puzzled at our appearances at their various locations, especially my appearance at the "white" locations. More rejections, of course, but this time, a lawsuit by yours truly ensued. The corporation settled the legal situation with my being able to rent a beautiful apartment in East Flatbush. Mine was the first Black Family in the building.

My two years of teaching at Nazareth were wonderful and unforgettable. Fifty-plus years later, I am still in touch with students. However, there was something tugging at me as an intellectual. I needed a bit more of a challenge, and I wanted to give something back to the Jesuits for the eight years of the free outstanding education they had given me. I was hired by another brave religious man to teach Latin and Greek at Brooklyn Preparatory School, which was located around the corner from the church in which I had been married with that rainbow of attendants. The environment there was much different from Nazareth, but as it turned out, I had a deep influence on those students too. So intense was this influence (clearly unknown to me at the time) that forty-nine years later, I was named an honorary alumnus with the pomp and ceremony that accompanies such an accolade from a Jesuit organization, albeit long "out of business."

It was not exactly only my instruction in Advanced Placement Latin which made an impression upon the boys of Brooklyn Prep. Similar to my time at Nazareth, I was the advisor/moderator of an extracurricular activity. At Nazareth, it was the speech and debate team; at Prep, the dance committee. There was a student-sponsored dance every eight weeks or so, plus the Senior Prom. My job was to keep the student chairperson focused and the till in the black, and maintain a Catholic social atmosphere. Building the confidence of the young student leader was a pleasure and a challenge. Little did I know such would have a lifelong effect! I was just doing my job—teaching. Dwight D. Eisenhower, the World War II General, and President decades ago, wrote, "A good teacher is one who can understand those who are not very good at explaining, and explain to those who are not very good at understanding." I believe that I was a very good teacher.

The announcement of the closing of Brooklyn Prep as well as our desire for a second child gave me an incentive to seek a type of job that paid many more dollars than teaching in a parochial secondary school. Long story shortened; I obtained a position with a major manufacturer of men's toiletries as a merchandiser, and was quickly promoted to salesman with a territory of $1 million in sales. When I left the company after eighteen months, sales had risen to $1.5 million. I was the first and only black member of the sales force of this national Boston-based company whose fame and name was (and still is) in blades and razors. This was a great job with a company car, travel allowance, and amazing medical benefits.

Our second child was a boy born on March 15, 1970, we named Peter (not a junior; we just liked the name). The birth cost us only the fee charged by the hospital for the use of the telephone for long-distance calls—under $2, as I recall. As stated, amazing medical benefits! The district manager even sent flowers to Laura upon the birth of our son. Much less drama and fear involved in this trip to the hospital! I proudly drove Laura, Elizabeth, and the soon-to-be-born baby to the hospital myself. No begging, no pre-pays, no discrimination! My black son was born in relative freedom, and was to live his entire life that way with perhaps one exception late in his senior year in high school, a few months prior to his entering college.

Unknown to me at the time, there was research being conducted with respect to the improvement of the academic performance of inner city youth, particularly high school students. A model for instruction had been created by an education scholar, and someone had found a local building in which to conduct this experiment. The Principal, a former Xaverian brother, had been selected, and a search was in progress for a black male Assistant Principal. A black male who had been raised in the ghetto, had been a teacher or administrator, and was a Catholic preferably. Somehow, my name came to the attention of the leader (a Xaverian brother, of all people) of this education experiment. I was found, interviewed a few times, offered the position, and took the job. I returned to the world of education, and this time, forever.

Chapter 11

Another Journey Begins:
Bedford-Stuyvesant and Wyandanch

The experimental secondary school for boys in the inner city of Brooklyn was named the New Catholic High School, led by yet another white male of Irish extraction, CF, with many of the same ideals and methods as Mr. R of CYO fame. The model ordained that the head of the school, the Principal, was to be totally in charge of the instructional program, and the Assistant Principal to be responsible for everything else. So in the fall of 1968, here I was, first and foremost in charge of the behavior of about 100 black teenage boys, responsible for the operation and security of the physical plant of a parochial high school (St. John's Preparatory) in its final year of existence, the buyer of all products and supplies, preparer of payroll, and director of athletics. CF put together a most interesting staff to administer instruction to these young men—a Xaverian brother (Science), a Franciscan brother (English), three nuns from different congregations (Math, Library, Guidance), a Hispanic layman (Social Studies), and young white Jewish woman (Spanish). In addition, there was a black gay male (Art); some paraprofessionals—some straight, some not so straight; and someone teaching physical education and health. This was quite a combination reporting to CF and yours truly, especially since none of them had ever had a Black boss or co-boss or assistant boss in their careers thus far. This was a first of a first!

To ensure some modicum of academic success for the students, many of whom had "rap" sheets, single or no parents, gang affiliations, and a myriad of social disorders and outside interests, each student was individually scheduled into what were called *mods* (modules), fifteen-minute segments of time as opposed to full forty-five-minute periods, which were the norm for education in the 60s. So José would have English for two mods, but Joseph would have math for three mods. It was a bit of a mess, but all of us got it. The students did well. Among this group, by the way, were two white kids, who also did very well academically and socially. That was amazing! But the school itself, later renamed the New High School, was amazing. An experimental secondary program located in the ghetto of Brooklyn, where I learned the importance of not only close connection with the student body but also immediate connection with the local NYPD precinct. There are several stories I could share at this point in my career, but allow me to tell this one.

We parked our automobiles in the street on the block in front of the school building. I had arranged with the City to have that part of curb to be so designated for us. Simultaneously, I had made arrangements with "the locals" not to disturb any of our automobiles during the workday—my car, especially, since it was the mode of transportation for the basketball team to get to "away" games. One day, it appeared that someone did not get the memo, and a battery was taken from the car of the Spanish teacher. So, upon her departure from the building this day, the car would not start. We determined quickly upon raising the hood that the battery was missing. I put the Spanish teacher into my car, and we drove to the local "chop shop" and purchased her battery—yes, the very battery which had been removed from her car. The agreement not to touch our automobiles was reinforced, and such never happened again, at least not while I was the assistant principal. An early lesson in negotiating with the enemy, or a throwback to my retail store union experience and/or funeral masses as an eighth grader! One difference—the power structure was Black street, not White Italian.

It seems that our instructional success reached well beyond the boundaries of Bedford-Stuyvesant, Brooklyn, into the eastern part of Long Island, and a state educational organization called the Board of Cooperative Educational Services (B.O.C.E.S.). Thus, among the many visitors we had to observe our experiment was a white official from this New York state educational agency who was so impressed with my work that he offered to place me in a public school district in Suffolk County called Wyandanch. The job, Director of Elementary and Secondary Education, was the equivalent to that of an Assistant Superintendent of Schools for Curriculum and Instruction.

Wyandanch, New York, a predominantly black-pupil-populated school district of about four-square miles, was located between two white suburban school districts in the center of the county. There were three elementary schools, an intermediate school, and a junior-senior high school. Education had come to a standstill years before I got there, and the state needed to see some improvement in the performance of the students (and the staff). Four of the five principals were white, and three of them resented me—the new and first black central office administrator— almost immediately. The junior-senior high school principal was a seasoned black educational professional hired at the same time with me. We worked well together in an attempt to make the students have an educational itch which they could (and would want to) scratch. From 1972 until 1975, I fought certain members of the board of education—both black and white, principals, and the State Education Department to establish stability and respect for what we were trying to accomplish for these urban/suburban students.

At some point during my New High School and Wyandanch assignments, I enrolled in graduate school at Hofstra University, became certified as a public school administrator, earned a Master's Degree in Educational Administration, bought a house, and moved the family to Uniondale, Long Island, New York. Ironically enough, my new next-door neighbor was a black lieutenant in the New York Police Department, Housing Division. We got along just fine! The move to Long Island was necessitated by the fact that I knew I could not raise my children in the city of New York with the same success that my mother had. I did not possess her skills, skills which I cannot name or define even fifty-plus years after her death. Elizabeth was 4; Peter was 1. Both children were formally educated there and graduated with honors from Uniondale High School, with Elizabeth attending Hofstra, and her baby brother attending Harvard.

Laura became active in the Parent–Teacher Association, eventually becoming President of the combined PTAs of all six or seven schools in the District. I believe she was the first person of color to achieve such a position, although the school system was about 20% Black at the time. This may be a good opportunity for me to share with you that one racial incident in the life of my son. The incident is a reminder that not just white people discriminate against black people. Some black people do the same thing. There is a national African American organization named after some storybook characters, whose mission it is to promote the success and advancement of Black youth. My son was at the top of his graduating class, and clearly eligible for this organization's annual scholarship award. My son, however, did not receive the award, which went to a black girl of a lighter hue and with both parents living in the household. Yes, Laura and I had become divorced by the time of our children's secondary school attendance.

During my work in Long Island, and my becoming single again, I decided that it was time for me to learn how people outside of the New York metropolitan area educated their children. I also realized that I had skipped a step in my administrative climb; being skipped in elementary school was enough for me. Oh, by the way, my son was also skipped in the early grades of his formal education. *The New York Times* Sunday Edition, offered several pages of advertisements for educational opportunities throughout the nation. Not wanting to be that far from my children, I applied for an administrative position in a place called Newark, Delaware. I did not get the job, but was called back a year later and offered the principalship of either one of two middle schools. I had never been away from New York as a full-time resident, and observing the wide-open spaces of first New Jersey, and then Delaware was an eye-opener. As I was to learn much later in life, there were even wider and more open spaces south of Newark (pronounced with pride *New Ark*). It was now the summer of 1975, ten years subsequent to my college graduation and first teaching job. I moved to Delaware with the help of the original owner of my first car (who was also the head usher at my wedding), and two of my former Nazareth students. Obtaining a one-bedroom apartment in a favorable location was fairly easy, probably because of the fact that I was hired by the school district, which had an affiliation with one of the local realtors. Ironically enough, the apartment complex was located on a street named Harmony Road. Peter E. Carter was about to become the first Black middle school principal in a suburban community of The First State. This was my first true educational leadership position in which I was the boss with a full staff of professionals and support personnel reporting to me.

Chapter 12

Meanwhile . . .

There are few tidbits that defy an actual chapter title and do not fit in anywhere in particular. Like, for instance, the death of my grandmother. While she was still alive and in her seventies, she had moved to Brooklyn to a three-story brownstone which she had purchased some years earlier. Despite her ornery disposition and personality, I used to visit her almost every Sunday, both when I lived in Brooklyn and when I lived in Uniondale. The visits were not necessarily very pleasant, but lucrative. I never left empty-handed, and when special needs arose, she wrote a check. Looking back on the encounters, I surmise that she felt extremely guilty for the manner in which she had treated her (now deceased) daughter and her grandson. The old lady even purchased an automobile. She neither knew how to drive nor possessed a license. In her mind, she expected that I would drive her wherever she wanted to go whenever she wanted to go there. That, of course, was not to (and did not) happen. She did manage to obtain the services of a "companion" who lived with and catered to her for years until her last day, which I did witness personally. I took care of the funeral arrangements via the same company which had handled my mother's passing. Grandma had an amazing devotion to St. Jude, the Patron Saint of Hopeless Cases. So devoted was she that she purchased a full-sized statue of St. Jude and donated it to the local parish Catholic church. At some point during their association, and this was bound to happen, the church and my Grandmother had a falling out. She had the statue removed from the church and placed in her bedroom, and surrounded it with candles, and some flowers now and then. That statue remained there for years and years. I returned it to the church with an apology after her funeral mass at that very church.

I inherited, no strings attached, the brownstone, and soon stupidly sold it for an amount well below its worth a mere ten years later. I just did not have the patience to deal with a house on Long Island and a rental property in Brooklyn. There were issues with the City of New York and a water line from their fire hydrant which was located at the curb in front of the house at 477 Bainbridge Street. In a sense, this was my second Beatles moment. Mistakes make one stronger and better, I have been told. My two judgmental errors deprived me of substantial income and wealth.

Studying for my postgraduate degree at Hofstra University was interesting, and not that difficult. The chair of the Educational Administration Department practically begged me to pursue a doctoral degree, informing me that if I were to ever become a Superintendent of a major American city (and he somehow saw that in my future), I would need such a trophy. I came very close, made the championship playoff, but not the Super Bowl. Many call me Doctor Carter anyway. All I needed was to pass a course in statistics and to write and defend a dissertation! I met a woman (PS) during my studies with whom I fell in love, and in everlasting friendship. I called upon her several times to assist me in many of my school leadership roles. She did make it to the Super Bowl, and, by the way, was married to some other joker for a while. So much for that, other than to document that she eventually was to play a major role in my daughter's finally obtaining her doctoral degree.

Chapter 13

Gauger Middle School:
Newark, Delaware

I had never met *rednecks* before the fall of 1975, and had no idea the extent of their dislike and actual hatred of those of us on the planet who were not White. Let me be clear, though, that the majority of the people with whom I was about to associate were not rednecks, but there were enough. I believe my first day on the job was at the beginning of August to get the school ready for the September opening. The school had been in existence for only five years with a "wall-less" concept for educating sixth, seventh, and eighth graders and headed by a scholar in the area of curriculum and instruction, but with no experience or knowledge of managing an institution of 1,200 *betweenagers* in square footage to accommodate 986 students. In addition there was an elementary school housed in the same physical plant. We had to use four elementary classroom spaces for half of our sixth graders. Recall that I stated that the building was constructed with as few actual walls between instructional areas as possible. This was the brainchild of some university types as well as the first principal. The staff was young and intellectually diverse, many with Southern accents. The Assistant Principal's nickname was

"Buck." Our students were drawn from a range of relatively expensive single-family homes to inexpensive trailer parks and affordable apartments. Ten to fifteen percent of the pupils had been classified as special needs, and I would say that about five of those children were just plain "nuts." I realize that such a designation is out of order for any professional educator to use, but *severely mentally handicapped* just does not capture who these individuals truly were. There were some mentally challenged staff members, too, starting with the woman who was my first secretary, who I was told was eventually institutionalized.

The custodial staff were all rednecks except the head of the physical plant. The cafeteria staff did their best to hide their feelings about a Black Principal. The teachers! Remember I described them as diverse in intellectual prowess. I was being kind. However, there were many talented individuals in the group of about 80. None had ever been this close to a black man before, except for one individual female who was black (and later became a gynecologist) and did not even like teaching, and definitely did not like me. Actually, very few of them liked me at the beginning, nor did they really like one another. Everyone was moving in his or her own direction. So, I united the staff by having them all agree that they disliked me for whatever may have been their individual reasons, some of which were, of course, racial. That strategy worked, and we eventually became a school. I bought some walls, separated the wheat from the chaff in terms of regular and special education, and demanded exemplary behavior on the part of the students and the staff.

The students were transported to school daily in about 20 buses, reminiscent of my CYO Day Camp days. We improved the behavior on those buses, too, given the socioeconomic population of the community each bus served. This in itself was interesting and challenging.

I have to honestly admit that this was a difficult assignment for yours truly, and little did I know that it was about to become worse. The state of Delaware was in the midst of federal court proceedings on the subject of racial desegregation of its northern schools. Very simply, the City of Wilmington, which was a majority minority-populated municipality, educated only its own pupils, while the 10 surrounding districts educated their predominately white suburban pupils. The case ended with a federal judge declaring the existing system unconstitutional (separate and equal, a no-no) and ordering all eleven districts to be merged into one. The effect of the court order on Gauger Middle School was that we would receive at least 200 seventh- and eighth-grade boys and girls from the city of Wilmington whom we would educate with our existing pupils. The court was clear in its ruling: No individual class would exceed an 80:20 White–Black ratio. There was no allowance for placement based on ability or achievement, just race. A federal monitor was assigned to the school to ensure that the court order as written was followed. He and I, of necessity, became fast friends.

The implementation of the August 5, 1977 court order took place in October of 1978. Prior to the actual implementation, there was a teachers' strike which lasted weeks in duration. Ninety percent of my staff was on the picket lines from early in the morning. Some mornings, I would buy and distribute donuts to them as they withstood the elements of weather. The strike was caused by the fact that teachers in the City of Wilmington were paid more than those working in Newark. The newly formed union was clear in its position that teachers working one classroom apart must be paid equally. Management did not necessarily agree, until about the Thanksgiving of 1978. It was essential that all concerned realize that the strike was not about integration of pupils, but about equity of pay of the teachers.

Many of us had been assigned to specific task forces in the year intervening order and implementation in which we worked laboriously to ensure success in the actual integration process. Eleven sets of board policies, for example, had to be scrapped and a brand-new policy (at least 300 pages) written. I was a member of this policy committee, chaired by one of the few black central office administrators, the former Superintendent of the Wilmington Board of Education. All the issues that dealt with teacher rights and responsibilities, including compensation, were raised during our deliberations, but we knew in our hearts and souls that a strike was inevitable. The President of the Teachers' Association insisted that the schools open on time, and hoped for a resolution given his concession not to strike before school opened. And, let's face it, he wanted to be sure his members received a paycheck or two before walking out. Schools opened in September as scheduled, and the teachers struck in the following month.

The strike ended, and school began in earnest. We attempted to meld and mold and blend the black kids from the City of Wilmington with the suburban (and redneck) kids of quasi-rural Newark. Prior to September, several of us worked assiduously to ensure as smooth a school opening as possible. In addition to the "administration" were rank-and-file members of the staff, two of whom became and remained my friends forever.

The first year, or should I say the first months of court-ordered desegregation were very difficult. The students from the city were in a new and unknown environment; the existing students were interacting with boys and girls about whom they had heard but never met. It was helpful to all concerned that the principal was a black male, since many of our challenges came from the black male students from the city and the white male students from the trailer parks. There were occasions when either I or my guidance counselor had to drive a student back home to Wilmington just to keep the peace for the day or the week. There were other times when we had to interact with student advocates from the city, whose goal was to ensure that the city kids were treated fairly. Those meetings tended to be contentious at times. A thousand thanks to my time in the low-income housing projects of Brooklyn as well as my time in Wyandanch, and a million thanks to ER, DG, RK, and TB, who were ever at my side. We survived the first year and the year thereafter, and indeed many years after that (long after I had left The First State). Lest we forget that our mission was to educate children, allow me to brag that achievement rose significantly during my time at Gauger, and that staff morale also rose to an all-time high. We were running on all eight cylinders, sometimes even more.

One of the highlights of this experience was the school's production of *Oliver* with an all-middle-school-student cast and orchestra. One of the parents, a dance professional, directed the show for us. It was great! We had an annual eighth-grade dance prior to June's promotion exercises. There were science fairs, Olympics of the Mind, fashion shows, and stock car races. We even attempted a spelling bee, although the principal had to be talked into that activity. Daily lunch occurred without incident; transportation was safe and steady, the corridors were clear during classes, the teachers were teaching and teaching well, the bathrooms were smoke free (for the most part), especially after I removed the outer doors. Interestingly enough, twenty-five or so years later, the architectural design for all pupil lavatories excluded the outer door.

Peter E. Carter received many accolades from the state (Governor), federal (monitor), and local (area superintendent) officials for my leadership work during the first years of court-ordered desegregation, and for my five years at Gauger in general. I was hopeful to receive a central office position for the fall of the 1980 school year, but the area superintendent felt that I was too good to remove as the principal of what became his star middle school. A much lesser qualified individual was appointed to the vacancy. A promotion earned and deserved, but not granted. I resigned my position as Principal, and moved to New Jersey to head a small suburban middle school. I also pledged to myself that if I ever reached the superintendent's level, never to deprive a promotion to a talented employee in order to maintain a certain status quo.

Oh, I almost forgot, I married for the second (and final) time while in Delaware. Okay, I did not really forget. My second wife was a wonderful young teacher who worked in one of the district's elementary schools, and who, of course, accompanied me to New Jersey, where she excelled as an educator in her own right, eventually becoming an elementary school principal. No conceptions, no births, a good marriage, and an amicable divorce! One could say that I was on an eight-year plan when it came to the nuptial experience.

Chapter 14

The New Jersey Ride Begins:
Franklin Middle School, Metuchen

We now begin the serious part of my progress to the goal for what was to become several touchdowns. A year prior, however, I experienced a very interesting and significant happening. I was interviewed in a suburban school district for the position of Assistant Superintendent for Curriculum, which would have been an unbelievable first for a black man (or woman). The Director of Personnel was impressed enough with my resume and initial interview that she moved my candidacy forward to the Superintendent of the school district, who happened to be a middle-aged Irishman. Naturally, I felt relatively comfortable with regard to a positive outcome. Such was not to be the case here, however. This was New Jersey in 1979, not Brooklyn in 1958. The superintendent, using the excuse that I was just too light (*light* meaning not enough experience) to be hired into the position. We all knew the real reason: He lacked the guts, for surely I did not perceive him to be a bigot. The respect the Director of Personnel (BW) had for me, and I for her, endured for forty-plus years, including my being a presenter at her retirement function, and years after that as a guest at her Florida home. The advice she gave me during my years as a school administrator in New Jersey remains invaluable to this day.

The superintendent of the Metuchen Boro Board of Education was a brave and brilliant Italian who challenged my skills almost on a daily basis, starting with his initial interview. GL was unique in his leadership skills, and I learned so much from him, quite similar to AF, another Italian for whom I worked in Wyandanch. Yes, it appears that I kept being surrounded by Catholic white males in my public school settings. The superintendent's offices were housed in the middle school to which I had been unanimously appointed as Principal. The great news about the position was that the school was scheduled to be closed in five years, giving me a preordained exit. Although I was the first black principal in this extremely suburban district, the staff was not totally a stranger to people of color. There had been a recent female Assistant Principal and was a current black male teacher. Of interest and of note, these two individuals were more white than black. The whole place was really run by a spinster math teacher who loved certain types of students, and disliked most adults, especially administrators.

Franklin Middle School educated 300 seventh and eighth graders; Gauger had a population of 1,200. The students, which included blacks from middle-class households, were virtually well behaved, although the staff leader and her followers did not think so. The school needed to become more a place for young teens than the quasi-penal institution that I met, and so I set about to humanize the place. To say that there was staff *resistance* to my changes is an underestimation and misrepresentation of the word. Most of them did not even like the child-oriented posters I placed on the walls of the corridors over a weekend. At my prior middle school, there were about seven fights a day during my first year which dwindled down to three fights per day during my second year, and none by the time the Governor of The First State visited the school to recognize our moving from worst to first as a middle school in Delaware. My rationale for the lack of teen physical conflicts in Metuchen, New Jersey, was that the students did not wish to mar their designer jeans in any way.

Middle school kids, especially those from upper middle-class households, are intrinsically evil, however. Begging forgiveness—not all! There was an occasion where a group of the wealthier set planted "Ex-Lax" tablets in the sandwich of a classmate who just did not measure up to their standards. Another student was harassed for not wearing a female support undergarment. The student victim happened to reside with her mother in a home for battered women, a situation anathema to several of the girls. Yes, it was the girls who tended to be a bit ornery, although in the instance just referenced, the victim was a bit of an aggressor in her own right. There came a point in time when a teen actor of a popular television soap opera and his parents opted to move to Metuchen. The basis of their buying a house in the community was that the train station (for easy transportation to Manhattan and the set of the television drama) was close by, and that the train station had potted flowers on the platform. I kid you not!

The students disliked this interloping actor with intensity, and let him know it in a variety of ways, not necessarily worthy of description. He was not the nicest of human beings, either. I solved this ongoing teen-created conflict by having a small group of students come to my office at 3:00 pm (airtime of the soap) to actually see their classmate on television. Instant stardom! The problem with the female student was solved too, yes, by purchasing the requisite personal items for the young lady in return for a reduction in aggression. Funny thing, though—the girl just did not like wearing bras. She told me so, personally! Speaking of attire, I had a rule which banned shorts of any kind at any time for both the boys and the girls. The boys challenged the equality of the rule, stating that the girls could wear skirts which may have been shorter in length than shorts. The Principal's retort was that the boys were welcome to wear miniskirts. One boy did just that one morning—the highlight of my career! He ultimately became a well-known author and filmmaker, and wealthy.

One final story about my leadership in the Brainy Boro (yes, they actually called it that) deals with the temperature of the building in which we educated the students. It was relatively cool in order to keep teen hormones in check. The Superintendent—remember, he was kind of my tenant—complained frequently about the lack of warmth in his office during the winter months, despite my explanation about the thermostat settings. I bought him a sweater and an electric heater. Problem solving was my greatest lesson during this assignment. One needs to inquire about the instruction at this middle school. The students performed very well, of course. They were white and suburban. I was able to even increase the performance data of my seventh and eighth graders while simultaneously helping them to gain an appreciation for the elderly as well as a caring for the less privileged. At the end of the five years, the Board voted to close the school as had been predicted, and I persuaded the realtors in town (there were seven) to give the staff a farewell luncheon on the last day of school. By the way, the Promotional Exercises, encompassing both grades, were outstanding. A few of those students and their parents and I became lifelong friends, including the straight miniskirt-wearing male student.

A funny thing happened on my way out of the door in 1985. The Superintendent inquired as to my next stop. I did not have one, actually, so he appointed me to a created position of Director of Intermediary Education to assist him with the transition of the districts' schools to a K-7, 8-12 configuration. He also gained warmth in his office from the building's furnace, and not the heater which he hardly used anyway. I enjoyed the warmer building in my new office too. During that school year, my former boss from the New High School, now in Concord, New Hampshire, lost one of his teachers, Christa McAuliffe, an astronaut in a tragic accident on the NASA spacecraft Challenger. My second wife had been hired as a teacher of middle grades in Metuchen, having spent some years prior thereto working as a manager for McDonald's. As mentioned earlier, she went on to become a Principal in the district—a second black, and a second Carter.

I spent that year learning from the master, GL. Until now, I believed the whole gestalt was about teaching and learning. At least I positioned myself in such a way to reinforce such a belief. During what we can call my apprentice year in the central office of a school district, I learned that educational leadership pertained to the successful manipulation of the politics of the area, and of the state. It pertained to the counting of votes, the granting of favors, and the building of a budget. That Board Member who just happened to drop by was not conducting a friendly house call, more of a witch hunt (in sheep's clothing) perhaps. And, ah yes, the Teachers' Association was as much a union as the one run by my "friends" at the retail chain in 1964. During this year of transition from building administration to central office, I practiced how to better interact with other principals, many of whom I considered less than adequately talented for the task. I was given the opportunity to attend several regional meetings where I met and listened to many other superintendents whose example was subtle, silent, smooth, and select. Becoming aware of some of the inner workings of the political system which drove education in New Jersey was fascinating. Little did I know that someday I was to become an integral part of that very system!

I applied for several positions, about twenty is my recollection—many potential firsts among them. I was eventually considered as a finalist for the position of Assistant Superintendent for Curriculum and Instruction in Irvington, New Jersey. It took the man who was to become my new boss, another brave Italian, by the way, three months to finally garner the required number of votes for me to become the first Black central office administrator in what was a predominantly minority-student school district. Fancy that: black kids, white administrators—; blacks need not apply! Peter E. Carter did apply and was hired to what was to become the beginning of his outstanding professional career and recognition.

Chapter 15

Irvington, New Jersey:
Its Board, Its Government, and Its Essence

It was the early spring of 1986 and I was sitting in a cubicle which was to be my office as an Assistant Superintendent. The entire central office of the school district was housed in what possibly had been a warehouse of some kind, or even a department store. The building was located on the main thoroughfare which joined Irvington to the state's largest city, Newark. All kinds of commodities were transported to and from daily. A few people had actual offices, one of whom was the board secretary, the most powerful white man in the town, perhaps in the world if one listened to others. I recall that during my final interview and handshake on the deal, the B.S. walked (no knock or anything) into the Superintendent's office, used the rest room, and on his way out, turned around and looked at me and said, "I'm _____. I pay your salary." Well, welcome to Irvington, Mr. Carter!

Next to my cubicle was the cubicle of the other Assistant Superintendent, a Jew. His nationality and heritage are important for several reasons. Irvington, prior to the migration of an African American population from the city of Newark, had been a predominantly Jewish and

Polish community. There were beautifully constructed and designed apartment buildings throughout the three-square miles which were this township. As the township became more black during the years, so did the buildings, so to speak. Over 60,000 souls lived here, stacked one on top of the other, with the exception of one part of town where there were some single-family homes. Eight thousand pupils attended the ten schools in the district, with 2,000 of them enrolled in the high school. I guess it was fortunate that only 1,800 attended on a regular daily basis. No, it wasn't.

To return to our cubicles, and my Jewish colleague! He had sought the top job, but "the other candidate" was chosen by a 5–4 vote of the nine-member Board of Education. He had been a principal of one of the elementary schools. The man who got the job—my boss—had been the director of one or more or all of the federal programs, and was clearly just a better school administrator and certainly a better human being. It was overly apparent that my cubicle neighbor resented the decision the board had made in his non-selection, and moreover very upset that this black young man had been hired as his equal. He never accepted the equal part, and spent much of his time just staring at me, and wondering what I was doing. In addition to that discomfort was the daily visitation of the President of the Board of

Education, a woman also of the Jewish persuasion who was hoping that Irvington would return to what it once was. Across from me sat another administrator, a white female and ally of the other assistant. The assistant's job description stated that he was in charge of personnel of the school district, a job actually done in part by this ally woman. So, there I sat, surrounded by racists and bigots and fools. Fortunately, there were five subject area supervisors who reported directly to yours truly, all of whom were very intelligent and diligent (for the most part). All five were crowded into a little office and worked very well together as well as independently. One of them also quietly did some of the personnel work for the aforementioned assistant.

Then there were the principals of the elementary [K-6] schools! These were talented and creative men and one woman who made it all work for the children in their schools. They worked independently of the central office administration, but were very polite and attentive at staff meetings, as I recall. They were also quite supportive of one another and made adjustments in pupil personnel as they saw fit, an unauthorized, but accepted practice in the district. We had a building that attempted to educate the town's seventh and eighth graders, also led by a very talented man, and then there was the high school, named after a man by the name of Frank

H. Morrell. The Principal of the 9-12 high school was married to the daughter of the county's Prosecutor, the only qualification he had for the job, or at least so it seemed. His talents were also unique—not great for kids, but different! The high school was to be the proof of the pudding, as I shall soon share. Did I mention that there were no black principals when I arrived in the spring of 1986? No matter, let us continue.

The State of New Jersey had been evaluating the academic success or lack thereof of its secondary school students with an instrument called the High School Proficiency Test (HSPT). Two weeks after my arrival in 1986, the statewide scores were published by the local press. Irvington High School had performed the worst (15.9% of ninth graders passed) on the math section of every high school in the state. Some weeks subsequent to this shameful news, a public meeting was held where the taxpayers (and others) had me for lunch and dinner, preceded by a flogging. I merely told the parents and other citizens not to judge me by these scores, but by next year's performances. The state reported in the spring of 1987 that 50.4% of the ninth graders had passed the math section. So significant was the gain that the department of education investigated the accomplishment. How could some black newcomer to this district get the scores up so high? The answer was simple: My

supervisors, my math guy (EY) especially—
totally immersed the students in their preparation
for the test, which was administered during the
winter months. We even involved the sports
coaches in our efforts to beat the HSPT. This was
one of many academic and instructional
achievements the district experienced under my
leadership and direction. I made believers of my
critics, bigots, and bosses.

The New Jersey Department of Education
was structured so that there was supervision over
the local school districts by a position known as a
County Superintendent. This position and the men
and women who held it was formidable. The
Township of Irvington was located in the County
of Essex, whose County Superintendent was a gay
Italian woman (ES) whom I dubbed with the title
of "*Educational Godmother*." I first interacted
with her when I represented Irvington and my
boss at one of the monthly meetings of the
county's district superintendents. She came up to
me at the end of the meeting, and quite pertly
asked, "Who are *you*?" I replied, "The Irvington
Assistant Superintendent," and the rest is
history—really good history. One example of the
positive interactions I had with this superstar of
an educational leader was the occasion when I
had to persuade her to approve an innovative idea
in the partial restructure of Irvington High School.
Quite simply (really not that simple), I had

identified a cohort of eighth-grade students who had not achieved ninth-grade status by virtue of their poor academic performances. I called the group Transitional Eight, or 8T, as it became widely known. They were moved forward to the high school, but not considered ninth graders. Approved!

I departed dear Irvington at what was the top of my game at the time. Not only was there noted improvement in the academic performance of the students, but also the athletic teams saw more Ws than Ls during my time there. Another state organization, the New Jersey School Boards Association, had been conducting a search for a superintendent of a small urban/suburban school district in Union County, New Jersey. One of the consultants of that organization had become acquainted with my work and recruited me for the vacant position of Superintendent of the Roselle Board of Education. I should have realized how contentious this assignment was going to be based on how I actually got hired. It was about the third interview and the board members were going back and forth about some trivial matter in the contract, causing me to politely excuse myself and walk out of the meeting. The Board Attorney, a Jewish woman, also left the meeting at a quick pace behind me, faced me in the corridor, and begged me to reconsider the offer if my terms were met. They were, and I did.

Chapter 16

Roselle, New Jersey: My First Superintendency

This place was not ready for a black school leader, even though there were some minorities on the board. There were two white men—one the mayor, another a taxpaying citizen who later gained a board seat—who were absolute bigots (actually probably White supremacists) who were to make my sojourn in Roselle extremely difficult. Some of the African American board members, one in particular, did not really appreciate my presence either. One saving grace was a terrific Italian-surnamed secretary (CS) whom I had hired, and we rode out the storm together. The other was the Union County Superintendent (VG)—yes, another Italian. Specifics are purposefully vague of my eighteen-month stay in Roselle, although we did get some good things done for the kids, despite the presence of a weak curriculum person and a sneaky business administrator. We bought the students textbooks, an entity seemingly lacking for years. The principals, two of whom were black, were of average talent, to say the least. One of those two was the high school principal, unfortunately. There were all sorts of allegiances and alliances in existence prior to and during my arrival in the district, none of which was beneficial to me. This was not a good place to establish a positive career, although I was again the first Black to hold the position. You may recall a certain Director of Personnel I met years before! She helped me through this period with words of advice and encouragement. In fact, I had consulted with her several times subsequent to 1980. Did I mention that she is Jewish? Her encouragement to stay the course would pay dividends beyond my imagination.

Removed from my immediate environment was a phenomenon known as a *state takeover* of a school district. A "takeover" was legally sought and enacted as a result of a district's inability or unwillingness to improve. The State was at the end of the process with respect to the takeover of the Jersey City Public Schools and appointed my Educational Godmother to be the State Superintendent of the district. She, in turn, highly recommended me to be her successor as the Essex County Superintendent of Schools, and I was so appointed by the Commissioner of Education and State Board of Education in the fall of 1989.

Chapter 17

New Jersey Department of Education: Essex County Office

The Office of the County Superintendent was located in East Orange, New Jersey, which housed several other state-operated entities. One of those other services was headed by a male Caucasian who could not at all fathom that a black man had been appointed to the position of Essex County Superintendent of Schools. He slowly and surely recovered from his initial shock, once he had tested my intelligence and capabilities. Also sharing space was a nonprofit student help group headed by a black female who welcomed my appearance in the building. Actually, I was her landlord, given the fact that my predecessor had given the agency some space gratis. I recall, too, a social work agency of some kind on the first floor of the building, an agency which had about four official automobiles. An automobile, separate from that fleet, was provided for the use of the county superintendent. My predecessor took her secretary with her to Jersey City, and I brought mine with me from Roselle. During my time in Roselle, I had the occasion to interview a business administrator who wisely declined that position. I hired him at the county office shortly after my arrival in my new position. I had my first administrative team: a Jewish male

(MD), an Italian-surnamed female, and yours truly.

A County office of education was a state-operated entity that monitored and mentored the needs of the local school districts within a particular county, of which there were twenty-one in the state. Each office was funded by the local county government, except for the salaries of the professional staff in each office. The clerical staff, supplies, equipment, and housing were the fiscal and physical responsibility of each county. Survival was dependent upon my relationship with the Essex County governmental officials. Such was tricky, but doable, with great reliance on my past experiences, some going back to those Brooklyn altar boy days and the retail store union encounter. The County always supplied my office with what it needed, including even a larger space in a new location, Cedar Grove, midway through my Superintendency. Our new office facilities were located on the grounds of the County's mental institution—no kidding. The relocation saved the County the cost of the rent for the East Orange address. Our work areas had been patient rooms; one room, in fact, had an all-iron door. However, there was a beautiful conference room, and the grounds were magnificent. We even had a colony of cats.

Unlike East Orange, which was urban, Cedar Grove was suburban—very suburban. Early on, I acquainted myself with the local police chief and his staff, allowing me smooth access in and out of the town. I recall an occasion when a state official who was black visited my office. He was followed into town by a patrol car, until it was clear that he was coming to Mr. Carter's office. Speaking of suburban towns in the Garden State, I travelled through a few of them to and from work. One particular afternoon while travelling on a major route during the busy commuter traffic, I was pulled over by a young white officer who claimed the reason for the "stop" was that I was driving erratically. In the type of traffic at the time, erratic driving would have resulted in an immediate colliding of two or more vehicles. The officer even summoned "backup" for his black male "stop" who was driving an automobile containing county government tags. The next day, his police chief verbally apologized to me for this incident.

Essex was one of the most populated counties in the State of New Jersey at the time, the most diverse, and sported very high budgets for its schools. Its diversity basically meant that it was home to the largest number of Blacks and Hispanics and Whites in the state. Needless to say, they did not live together in any of the same twenty-three school districts, with the exception of two. On the eastern end of the county were the minority students; the western end educated the wealthy and the white. I was the educational czar of both ends as well as the middle. Imagine if you will, twenty-three district superintendents having to report to one black man, who was a tough and arrogant SOB. One had to assume such a mantle in order to be effective in this county, and thus ensure the children received the type of education they deserved. The superintendents were diverse in their ethnicities and genders, and also tough individually and collectively. I represented the Commissioner and the Governor (regardless of political party affiliation) with the full support of a State Board of Education, which set the regulations, and the State Legislature, which set the laws. Each school district retained the services of legal counsel; my lawyer was the Attorney General. The wise and the worthy and the worldly among the district superintendents did not mess with their state "boss."   I should mention that during my six years in the job, two of them did attempt to defy yours truly, and those two (one a Jewish male, another a black female) lost their respective jobs. Peter E. Carter was one bad-ass "mother" and one of the four most powerful black men in the State. In fact, for a while there he was the most powerful black man in the State.

I had an office staff of about ten, five professionals, five clerical, although that number would vary by plus or minus two from year to year. Our job was to ensure that the rules and laws were being obeyed by the school districts and their personnel. My staff, diverse in race and gender, was interesting in that they had become used to and somewhat fond of my predecessor. Only one of them had a thing about being directed by a black man, but learned how to live with it. Together, we made Essex County a good place for children to receive an education, whether at the eastern or at the western ends. One of our many responsibilities was the certification of the professional staff in the districts. We were vigilant in spot-checking credentials, and from time to time discovered irregularities. Several improperly assigned staff members were either removed from their positions or from a district itself. There was even an incident with a substitute teacher in one of the districts who introduced voodoo during her teaching activity; I took away her certificate forever. There was a principal in one of our suburban school districts who lacked the proper credentials to so serve; she was duly removed to the shock and anger of the local superintendent and many of her supporters.

Other than the major accomplishment which shall be shared soon, there were several other contemporary incidents which bear mentioning. During my days on the job, a tree fell in the parking lot of a school, fatally injuring a principal; a roof caved in onto a classroom—no injuries; an elementary school burned to the ground during the Christmas holiday; eighth graders from every part of the county who had distinguished themselves in community activities met one another for an annual luncheon; and law enforcement and school leaders also broke bread together on an annual basis. I intervened in a dispute between students and their superintendent over a sketch involving condoms, supported an award for a piece of pupil sculpture involving condoms, and advocated for the provision of condoms to students at the County College. We raised the awareness of our superintendents with regard to child abuse, and I exposed them to the realities of the Holocaust through a survivor, the President of the State Board of Education.

The largest city in the State, Newark, was located in Essex County; it was also the largest school district. For years, the academic performance of the thousands of students who attended the Newark City public schools left much to be desired. Actually, I am being too kind; the performance was downright poor. The physical plants had been neglected, but the teacher and administrative salaries were plump. In fact, the superintendent had an outdoor ninth-floor patio attached to his office, and a car and driver for his use, 24/7. The Board of Education was elected, in a manner of speaking, although my investigations produced evidence of votes cast by citizens who had neither actually visited the polls nor cast an absentee ballot. The President of the Board was afforded certain accoutrements, including a laptop, a spacious office, and transportation. The Commissioner and State Board filed suit for the "takeover" of the school district of Newark. As County Superintendent, I was to play a major role through a process called Level III Monitoring and a Comprehensive Compliance Investigation, in which personnel from all 21 county offices were involved under my leadership.

The process was long and tedious, and even extended into another administration of an opposing political party. Fortunately, county offices were not often affected by politics (with emphasis on the word "often"), so we plodded on with our work. Each and every one of the 80 school buildings was visited; all personnel records were checked; and the spending practices and budget were examined with the proverbial fine-tooth comb. After several months, we felt secure in our findings, showing that Newark was unwilling and unable to improve, and thus needed to be taken over by the department of education. We shared same with a Deputy Attorney General who represented the plaintiff. The judge ruled in the case [Contini v. The Newark Board of Education] in our favor. It was April 1995.

Twenty-two years later, the state was to return the district to local rule, but that is material for another time, perhaps even another book.

A group of state department officials and a reporter who had been covering this for years were huddled in a small office close to 2 Cedar Street, the headquarters of the Newark Board of Education. Upon notification of the ruling of the judge, we marched over to 2 Cedar Street and literally took over the operations of the Newark Public Schools, having the superintendent escorted out of his office, and out of the building. This was a very touchy situation! The next steps for many days involved retrieving items from the board members (each of whom had an office, by the way), cancelling credit accounts at several local restaurants, and properly administering the budget of some $500,000,000. (yes that's $500 million). We had retired, but armed, state troopers to assist us in the retrieval of now state-owned property. These were dangerous days, including some negative remarks in the press from outgoing Newark administrators. I had to remove some other supervisory personnel from their positions for reasons of non-certification, one of whom later became the Essex County Executive. Eventually, a State Superintendent was hired for Newark, relieving me of a day-to-day onsite presence, thus allowing me to consider new professional options.

As the County Superintendent of Essex, I also served as a board member of the County College for six years, where I gained a great deal of knowledge about higher education. I was not only a board member but also the Chair of the Personnel Committee. There was an occasion in which I had to rule on the continuation of an employee on the payroll. The employee happened to be the mayor of the city, making his removal a political firecracker. The President of the College, a brilliant administrator of African descent, counseled me against making what I considered the proper recommendation, given that the mayor did not really teach any classes. The College President shared the spotlight of New Jersey black male leadership with me, and in fact was even more revered than yours truly. At one point, I served as Vice President of the Board and thus a member of the five-person county group (board of school estimate) to approve the annual budget. A controversial issue was a raise for the college staff. I was the swing vote, and was literally sought after by both sides. The budget was approved with the salary increase included. We met as a board once a month, with amicable and positive results. I also successfully advocated that the college's medical office stock condoms for the taking (no questions asked), especially on Friday afternoons prior to the weekend. I wanted to keep the college students, the majority of whom were Black, safe and alive.

As with most institutions, the College had a cafeteria where meals and snacks were sold. There came a point in time when it was apparent that the food operation was in the red— continually in the red. I offered the opinion (the correct one) that food was walking out the door. Surveillance cameras were installed at my insistence, and we recorded packets of meat being loaded into the trunk of a car of one of the cafeteria employees. We fired four of them; the books balanced, and then were in the black as they should have been. I may have failed to mention that the College was located in the eastern part of the County of Essex. The sociology dictated that the majority of the non-professional help were at the poverty line, and were sometimes tempted to seek criminal means to supplement their basic incomes. This type of theft was unfortunately becoming commonplace in the local public schools as well.

Interestingly enough, there were other colleges in the east, including Rutgers College of Arts and Sciences and Rutgers Medical School as well as the New Jersey Institute of Technology. All of these institutions were prestigious academic bastions of higher education, attended by a predominance of white students, and staffed by a majority of white adults. Essex County College, a two-year institution, negotiated acceptance of its graduating students by Rutgers for the students' remaining two years of higher education. This was quite an achievement of which we were all proud.

Twenty-three school districts and a college under my leadership for a six-year period, my longest lasting job—not bad for a Black man of 51 years of age!

Chapter 18

A Mental Pause

You will not believe the next stop on my journey of blackness, so we need to take a little breather in the chronology before we get there. I alluded to a few interactions with members of law enforcement, and here is one more. I was driving north on the New Jersey Turnpike one afternoon, again in heavy traffic, and was pulled over by a New Jersey state trooper. He had absolutely no reason for the "stop" other than the color of my skin, which, as this book's title states, is Black. Fortunately, over the years, I had accumulated a number of what we call "Driving While Black (DWB)" cards, given to me by the aforementioned VG, his son, and—of all people—a lieutenant of the New Jersey State Police whom I met at Newark Airport. The lieutenant was on her way to her mother's funeral, as I recall. I engaged her in conversation and referenced a superior of hers with whom I had interacted on another occasion. Our conversation ended with her giving me her business card, the upper righthand corner of which displayed the trooper logo. As I displayed my driver's license to the trooper who had stopped me, I was sure to also display the logo on the lieutenant's card. The words "I am so sorry, Mr. Carter, I made a mistake" were uttered immediately upon the viewing of the logo. I carry at least two DWB cards with me at all times.

Being in a supermarket or retail store was usually a negative experience. There were two stores in particular where upon my entry or being present for more than two minutes, the public address system beamed out a "code" message indicating that I needed to be watched. After a third time of this phenomenon, I knew it was not a coincidence. After a meeting with store and regional management, the electronic harassment ceased. Shopping in general was often interesting for me as a black man. Many times, store clerks whose salaries were significantly less than mine would either query as to the sincerity of the intent of a purchase, or attempt to direct me to an item of lower cost and decreased value. One exception was my interaction much later in life with a Mercedes-Benz sales manager from whom I purchased an SUV within thirty minutes of our encounter. Jewelry store clerks were a bit of a mixed bag, most keeping the extremely fine and very expensive pieces locked in their display cases, until I demanded the level of service I deserved.

Another most annoying situation is the stare from a white person (usually over 60) in a restaurant or other eatery where I am the only black about to dine or order a salad. I am not sure if I was the first and only African American they had ever seen up close or if they thought I was in the wrong restaurant, or perhaps I had no tongue or teeth. The looks and the stares continue depending on the nature of the venue. Of note, though, such is never the case in four- or five-star restaurants. I guess the other patrons believe that I am a professional athlete or show business personality. I do (or did) resemble Denzel Washington.

As part of the pause, I must mention my amusement as white people make decisions as to whether to enter an elevator with me, or sit on a commuter rail line next to me, or even make a friendly comment after a concert or book signing. It is rare that I ever ask a white woman to dance, so no problem there, gentlemen. By the way, attending white social events as a black man is extremely difficult, unless you are accompanied by a black woman. The attendees just feel more comfortable, I guess. Even greater joy and comfort permeates a room whenever I attend with my multi-degreed and attractive daughter. There is just something scary about a black male standing, or even sitting alone.

Last but by no means least, allow me to deal with the phenomenon of being made to feel invisible. This occurs usually in a line for any reason in which a person of an opposing race merely maneuvers to get ahead of me for whatever the reason. Or the person in front of me on his/her way out of a door allows the door to freely close in my face (although I have noticed that whites also do that to other whites). The best example of invisibility is during a conversation with, let's say, an attendant of some kind; the other racial person just bursts into the verbal interaction to ask their own question. Clearly, not only was I invisible but also my verbiage was of no import or value. To paraphrase the Roman author, Cicero, I shall pass over in silence the non-response altogether on those occasions when I dare share a greeting of the day with a white stranger.

Thus far, I am certain that we can all agree that life could have been worse, much worse for me as a black man. It was fortunate that I was able to attend very good schools which afforded me the same or even better education as my white male counterparts. Armed with such outstanding knowledge, I could only prosper as a professional, and as a black person. I know what they know, understand what they understand, and learned what they learned. Yes, I am Black, grew up extremely poor, but was very ambitious. I realized that I could accomplish a great deal as long as I kept my eye on the prize, and worked very hard. I worked so hard in fact that I suffered a heart attack (coronary artery disease) at 50 years old which I obviously survived, leaving only the right side of my heart fully operative with the assistance of three stents. The cause of the heart failure was primarily McDonald's cheeseburgers on a regular basis for lunch and little to no exercise. Fortunately, I had stopped smoking cigarettes on January 1, 1989, years prior to the cardiac incident. The cardiologist who treated me upon discharge from the hospital advised me to "stay away from stressful situations." Strangely, I thrive in stressful environments and situations.

By way of introduction to this next chapter, I need to remind you that as the County Superintendent, I had been conducting quite a bit of oversight with regard to one of my former workplaces. I received a call from the current Board President asking me to return as the Superintendent, an offer which I immediately turned down. One week later, he called again, stating, "Do it for the kids, not for us." As in the Tom Cruise movie, *Jerry Maguire*, he had me at *kids*. So here I went back (a no-no for most endeavors) to Irvington, New Jersey, as its Superintendent into a very stressful situation.

Chapter 19

The Return to Irvington, New Jersey

It was a bit surreal to return to the district where I had made my mark as an innovator and curriculum leader. It was the district that had given me my start and name as someone who was on his way to prominence in the State of New Jersey. Having gained that prominence as the County Superintendent, political and academic wisdom would have dictated a move away from what really had been my past. But I had something to prove, something to show, namely, that an urban school district educating black and poor kids need not be rated at the bottom of the achievement barrel. Little did I know that during my almost eight-year absence, so much bad had happened, and so much good had not happened.

My employment package was a good one—salary, benefits, conferences, car allowance, vacation days. The board at my time of hire was reasonable, the mayor was supportive, the police department cooperative, and the teachers' association (the union) cantankerous. Many of the principals with whom I worked as an assistant were no longer in those positions, but in some cases had been replaced by their assistant principals. There were still 8,000 pupils living in four square miles in multifamily dwellings headed by single females. Unfortunately, not much had been done to continue the outreach we had begun in order to assist the families with parenting skills, so that aspect of district interaction had to be renewed. Last, but by no means least, the district had accumulated an eight million-dollar ($8,000,000) deficit.

My first order of business was to promote the best principal (WR) to the position of Assistant Superintendent. I needed someone to run the place on a day-to-day basis. He was outstanding in his new position, and we became and remained friends for years and years thereafter. The leadership of the district had left much to be desired over the years. My immediate predecessor was just plain stupid. I wish I could describe him in a more diplomatic or courteous manner, but I cannot. The reigning Assistant Superintendent, who aspired to the job I was given, was insane (again, apologies for the blunt and possibly inaccurate adjective), and the existing Business Administrator was corrupt, and eventually went to jail—as did the mayor, by the way. The Assistant eventually left, having received a job as a Superintendent in one of the state's southern counties, where she was to be arrested and convicted of shoplifting in a local grocery establishment. Meanwhile, back at the ranch, the natives were restless. All the natives—

students, parents, teachers, board members, and lawyers!

So where does this black school leader begin to tackle this almost impossible situation? You cannot run an enterprise without money, so at the top of my agenda was the deficit. Let us be clear here. The district's audit showed Irvington in an eight-million-dollar shortfall situation. Over a two-year period, the district had spent money it had not taken in as revenue. The largest expenditure in an organization is payroll. Thus, there had to be drastic adjustments in this area. I announced to all during the first August weeks of my administration that would be "fewer people working here in June than work here now." And, yes, there were fewer people on payroll by the end of the following June, and the beginning of the next school year—a lot fewer people.

In many school districts, there are *patronage* jobs doled out to friends of and relatives of, and lovers of already-ensconced people on the payroll or on the board or in the town. There was quite a bit of money there. Then there were duplications in actual staff positions. As I visited the offices and schools, I was known to ask the question of an employee, "What do you do?" A hesitant or untrue reply would result in an imminent termination. I led by example in terms of a one-year salary freeze; the principals and supervisors association cooperated by agreeing to have their salaries likewise frozen. I cannot recall whether the Teachers' Association was able to also take such a position, but something was amiss because we had a teachers' strike. As I recall, the work stoppage (a "sick-out") was over lack of heat in the middle school, not necessarily wages, although there was a teacher demonstration at a board meeting led by their association president waving a dollar bill as she pranced down the aisle. It was quite something!

Then there were the inner workings of the business office where I had hired a new business administrator, a very intelligent and honest white woman, somewhat to the annoyance of the current business staff. During my time, I discovered that the Comptroller had not been sending the employee withholding taxes to the federal government. Since he was a family man, I spared him actual arrest, and merely fired him. I removed another staff member for the improper supervision of one of the females under his direction; oh, yes, she was terminated soon thereafter, too. No, I was not the most popular person in the district. Even my own secretary was trying to undermine me. These were interesting times!

The district had contracts with a myriad of vendors and agents for a variety of services. One such agent had been providing some type of undefined insurance for the district at an annual premium of some $10,000. Since no one, including the agent, could determine what this insurance provided, I cancelled the policy. The agent happened to be the President of the Senate of the State of New Jersey. A dangerously bold move indeed that I would make again, if necessary. You cannot take money from kids and give nothing back in return.

This is just a piece of the Irvington experience—an overview, as it were. Coming up shall be the real "nitty-gritty" of this adventure, which had begun October 1, 1995. The district had been what was called a Type I school district, in which the mayor appoints the school board members. As a result of a November 7, 1995, election, the district was converted to a Type II, expanding the board from seven to nine members, and making it an elected (not appointed) body. It was a nine-member elected board of Irvington citizens who met some years later during an annual conference in New Orleans, Louisiana, and decided to non-renew the superintendent's contract. I raise this fact in advance of the upcoming pages only to set the atmosphere and climate in which I had to work in order to improve the instruction for Irvington's 8,000-plus students. My mission was to have the pupils intellectually stimulated, instructionally challenged, and emotionally motivated to visually display and mentally portray their own unique gifts and talents as offered by the Board of Education.

Prior to my arrival as Superintendent, but during my tenure as County Superintendent, the Irvington School Board and Administration had embarked on a major 50-million-dollar capital program including additions to two schools and the building of a third. One project, the expansion of a middle school, had been completed with the exception of seismic bracing, an architectural and State requirement. Upon investigation, it was discovered that there were two sets of drawings, one (with the bracings) sent to the State, another (without bracings) actually utilized in the construction process. Thank goodness for one of my leaders from the Newark Comprehensive Compliance Investigation (CCI) unit who upon our joint inspection discovered the omission. An easy fix, one would think! And it was, as long as there were construction people to do the work. Small problem: The money for the project had been exhausted. In another smaller project, a new alleged state-of-the-art HVAC system failed. Last, but by no means least, construction on the new elementary school had ceased. The workers had been pulled from the job due to lack of payment to the contractor by the district.

I walked into an impossible situation with a myriad of, let's call them, questionable players. There was the president of the Construction Company (and his son, the vice president); there was the construction manager (a former mayor of a neighboring city) and his assistant; there were certain board members with guilt on their faces and possibly in their bank accounts. So we have $50 million for a $40-million-total project, and all the money has somehow been spent. I was determined to have all the construction completed within the next nine months of my taking the helm. Needless to say, it was imperative that I meet with the president of the construction company. A breakfast meeting was set up in a local diner. In attendance were said president, his son, his driver, my assistant, and yours truly. The driver had similar attributes to the gentlemen who tipped me after a funeral when I was an altar boy in Brooklyn, and the construction president reminded me of several of the men who populated the Italian section of my elementary school neighborhood. Once again, that childhood experience was to be a boon in my adult career. The district owed the construction company a few million dollars, and we needed some more millions to complete the project. The meeting was a bit contentious, to say the least, especially when one considered the bulge under the left side of the driver's jacket, but it ended with the president agreeing to return his men to the job "for the sake of the kids." And, I, in turn, agreed to come up with some money—a lot of money. During the meeting, I had no idea how I was going to get the money, a reality loudly emphasized by the son.

Spending six years at the Department of Education as a highly respected administrator was about to pay off in spades (pardon the color reference). After several carefully placed telephone calls, I was able to get a major advance on state aid direct deposited into the school district's account. This was an unprecedented act on the part of government, a first, giving a loan, so to speak, to a school district. Almost simultaneously, the premium for the employees' medical insurance in the amount of $500,000 became past due. So serious was this situation that the insurance company sent a vice president to my office to announce that the policy would be cancelled within 48 hours of our meeting unless a check was received in the full amount. A cancellation of the policy would have resulted in all of the district's employees losing their coverages immediately. A check in full payment was hand-delivered to the firm in 24 hours.

There were many interesting aspects to the deficit which I inherited as superintendent, one of which was the amount. The initial amount shown by an auditor and reported to the press and the public was a $6.8 million shortfall in 1993-94; the actual amount was, as stated earlier, $8 million due to several outstanding bills which had not been paid in 1994-95. In addition to staff reductions and the "loan" from the State, I also sought to recover almost $4 million in interest being held by the municipal government. It was interest earned on an initial $49.5 million deposited into the town's coffers for the school construction fund. Yes, there were many hands in the broth and in the porridge.

The August following my arrival was the arrival of an FBI agent. The previous month, the U.S. Attorney's Office in Newark had subpoenaed all of the district's financial records dating back to 1990. On the lighter side, the FBI agent was female and attractive, giving wonder as to where she kept her firearm. Since none of us was stupid, we never asked, but still wonder to this day. The FBI spent months at the district offices and found nothing illegal—no crime. What did occur, unfortunately, was additional evidence of greater hits to the ballooning deficit. Fortunately, the steps I had taken to reduce current spending were working. Miraculously, there were no initial increases in the local tax levy, keeping the citizens relatively calm, and through frequent public communication, we were able to gain the support of the majority of the community for what we were trying to do.

In about two years, the true deficit of $9.8 million was reduced to $1.8 million through the measures already stated. The Department of Education was breathing down our necks to eliminate the total deficit. The only method remaining was to raise the $1.8 million through a special tax levy to be collected during the 1997-98 school year. The road to Damascus and fiscal solvency was laden with ruts, roots, and ridicule. With bruises and blisters, we arrived at the destination with some wear remaining on our sandals. When my contract expired in June of 1999, the district enjoyed a $3 million-dollar surplus. Yes, I had turned the fiscal situation around by a full $12 million dollars–plus. In appreciation, the Board fired me.

During my tenure as the chief school administrator, one of our buses slid sideways into a toll plaza on New Jersey's Garden State Parkway. Three students, the bus driver, and a school aide were treated for minor injuries. Two weeks after the accident on or about May 20, 1997, an armada of New Jersey State Police, led by the number two person in the law enforcement community, descended without warning (and without invitation) upon the Irvington bus garage. In total, there were ten troopers (two of which were sergeants), two members of the vehicle inspection team, and the Captain. The call from the bus garage came into my office at about 2:15

pm, the same time that the Troopers ceased all transportation operations. The few buses which were on the road at that time were boarded upon their arrival at the garage, and the drivers' credentials checked. The challenge was that there were about 300 students who needed transportation back to Irvington from their special schools. I called upon one of my colleagues, who dispatched her buses to get our kids. The State Police occupied the Irvington bus garage for two weeks, inspecting every vehicle from horn to engine, and every piece of paper. The outcome was a total upgrade of our transportation department. The cause of the accident, by the way, was determined to be faulty brakes.

There were many instructional achievements, lest we forget why I was there in the first place. Significant increases were gained by the students in their statewide tests as well as on their quarterly school report cards as a result of better teaching methods. We added courses which were more in keeping with the needs of the students in terms of school-to-work. The Department of Education certified the district, moving it from Level II. Getting "on the good foot" with the department was essential to demonstrate that urban students could perform, and to ensure our continuing good standing for increased State Aid. We laid the foundation for the inception of all-day kindergarten instruction as well as half-day for four-year-old children. The co-curricular activities in the middle schools were strengthened in order to increase the motivation for learning of those students.

The new elementary school was built at one of the township's busy prostitute corners and had a large open area surrounded by glass. The classrooms too had large-size glass windows. I asked the Police Chief to discourage the traffic at least during school hours. White men would drive by slowly during the morning hours and transact business on a daily basis. The police department appeared to be unsuccessful in its attempt to alter the commerce. Yours truly had to have a conversation with the controlling "gentlemen" who were in high school when I was the Assistant Superintendent, and they kindly moved their stables one block over. No pain, no foul! Thus, the children could concentrate on their classroom activities without the distraction of adult street business, and the sun could still shine into the building.

In the spring of 1998, an arsonist set fire to the art room in the high school. The fire destroyed the room and prompted the evacuation of 1,800 students. The press reported, "About 20 firefighters worked to bring the blaze under control in Room 605", which is the classroom of teacher Rita Owens, the mother of actress and rap star Dana Owens, better known as "Queen Latifah." I had the distinction of handing a diploma to the young Miss Owens upon her graduation from Irvington High School. She was quite the athlete at the time, by the way. Through the skill and magic of my Assistant Superintendent working in tandem with the insurance company, the art room was restored beyond recognition and later renamed in honor of Mrs. Owens.

The middle school was located on the corner of Myrtle Avenue and University Place in Irvington. For years, it had gone by the name of the Myrtle Avenue School, carrying with it a not-so-favorable reputation. Pupil behavior was bad; pupil achievement was worse. Many attempts, including single-gender classroom education (not my idea, I assure you), were made to improve the tone and tenure of the school for the seventh- and eighth-grade African American students who attended school daily. Nothing seemed to change the climate and the reputation. So, Peter E. Carter changed the name of the school, with full board approval, to University Middle School. The dedication ceremony on June 22, 1999, was the final event of his leadership role as Superintendent of Schools. The change in name did wonders for the image of the school.

From the beginning of my career, I dreaded the thought and the reality of a child dying during my watch. As a principal in Delaware, there was a female diabetic eighth grader whose diet needed to be closely monitored. We shared those requirements with her classmates, who saw to it that she ate what she needed to and avoided what could kill her. One day, it so happened her mother called the school to inform us that her daughter was ill and was being allowed to stay at home for the day. The parent went off to work. When she returned home at the end of the workday, she found her daughter dead. She called the police, then she called the school to thank us for having kept her daughter alive. Even though the student died at home, I still felt that I had lost one of my kids during school hours. About twenty years later, while in Irvington, I did lose a student. It was almost dismissal time at one of the schools, and the children were enjoying outdoor recess with their principal and teachers. In the course of a softball game, one of the eighth-grade boys hit the ball sufficiently well to allow him to reach first base and then run on to second base. Upon reaching second base, the young man collapsed and was rushed by ambulance to the hospital, where he was pronounced dead. I, of course, went to the hospital, too, where the attending physician told me that the young man of 14 years of age had suffered a massive heart attack, and was dead before he hit the ground as he approached second base. It was I who had to tell his mother upon her arrival at the hospital that her son had died at school. I shall never forget her words to me as we viewed his corpse together: "I'm sorry, Mr. Carter. I meant to take him to the doctor." Of all the trials and tribulations I had endured as Irvington's Superintendent, this was the worst. I had lost a child on my watch.

As we close out this chapter and phase of my career, I must mention that I had become Vice President and then President of the New Jersey Council of Education, a most prestigious organization in the state, and—yes—its first African American President. I also enjoyed being President of the Essex County Superintendents' Roundtable (the group of all the county's school leaders which met monthly) while I was the Irvington Superintendent. I had also purchased a former vocational school from the county which came to serve as both the Superintendent's offices as well as a new school called Central Six, housing the grade level for which it was named.

The summer of 1999 was peaceful and restful as I enjoyed banking my unemployment insurance funds as well as the dollars accrued from my unused vacation days. I was in ecstasy! Ah, not so fast, Mr. Carter. The powers that be would not allow me to rest and be comfortable for longer than a few months. The son of VG, a school board attorney of some renown, highly recommended me to be hired as the chief school administrator of one of Passaic County's extremely suburban districts. During the process, I suggested that the board be informed as to what my parents may have looked like, lest there be any surprises. They were so informed, and I became the first (and probably only) black superintendent of this district which prided itself on no traffic lights, no sidewalks, and black bears (yes, real four-legged bears) of all ages. The people were White, rich, and Republican.

Chapter 20

Just Before the End

In more traditional biographical works, there is a preface that takes care of the general housekeeping which is to follow, but I find it just as appropriate to include those types of remarks as a penult in my narrative. My darling daughter, Dr. Elizabeth Ann Carter, gets the first appreciative mention for were it not for her persistence for many years, this book would never have been written. She even offered to be the scribe of her father's dictation should such ease the burden of authorship. Her insistence heightened when during a visit to my basement, she saw the hundreds, nay thousands, of pages of information which form my professional life, and which have served in many ways as the framework of this book. She is important most of all, though, for what she said to me in the spring of 2004: "Daddy, you have done enough. Retire." Greater love than that no man hath, nor woman, nor child.

The second catalyst and cause of this outcome is the current President of Fordham University, the Reverend Joseph M. McShane of the Society of Jesus. We had maintained a casual correspondence over the years, and during one of the recent exchanges, I had mentioned one of my firsts as a Black male. He casually (kind of) wrote back that there were probably several, and I should write about them all. Thank you, Fr. President, for that final push! As an extension of this acknowledgement, allow me to mention the Jesuits from college and high school who formed me into becoming the outstanding professional about whom you have read so far, with some more to come.

There were several women, some of color, some of not; some of love, some of not; all of influence and care. Laura and Florence get the prize for having the ability to have lived with me and loved me and supported me for eight years each, and who retained the name Carter even after divorce. There are yet others whose names have either appeared as initials or not at all who assisted greatly in my ascent to success.

You will notice that with just about three or four exceptions, there are no full names utilized in the book—just initials when someone of note needs to be mentioned. Only the first names of some of my teenage friends have been used, and, of course, such was done on purpose.

When I deemed it appropriate, I did resort to specific ethnic backgrounds of individuals in order to cast a contrast of one type of White person with another, or even a similarity. No apology is required for this essential literary license. In fact, as you read the book, one could see why such needed to be the case.

The last name to be mentioned needs no introduction, as she has been the backbone of the entire narrative, and without whom, both literally and figuratively, there would not have been Peter E. Carter, A BLACK FIRST. Bernice Mildred Camilla Carter, this book is for you with love! Thanks for being there on earth for the first 21 years of my life, and in heaven for the rest!

Chapter 21

Ringwood, New Jersey: The Final Frontier

The first thing I felt when I arrived in Ringwood in October of 1999 was a drastic decrease in the outdoor temperature. Ringwood is one of the towns in New Jersey at the southern border of New York State, and ten degrees colder than the temperatures in central New Jersey. As it turned out, only the temperatures were colder; the people of Ringwood were amazingly warm. At the utmost of my priorities was to communicate with staff and community, especially with the Board of Education. I initiated a publication called *InfoShare* which I promulgated regularly to the board, keeping each and every member apprised of happenings in Trenton, the state's capital, as well as my suggestions for continual improvement of the district.

One of the first matters of business was the procurement of social studies textbooks for the sixth-grade students, and eventually new textbooks across all the grade levels in the basic skills subjects. There was some push-back on the issue of textbooks by some board members, but eventually we all rested on the same page, and the students were the fortunate beneficiaries. I also had security systems installed in all the schools to better screen visitors upon their arrival at each school. I was somewhat surprised when I learned that this suburban school district with a pupil population of about 1,400 was lacking in teaching and learning, and security instruments.

The Borough of Ringwood has no sidewalks, thus forcing parents to transport their children via automobile to a playdate, a ballet class, a karate lesson, grandma's house, or for an ice cream cone. Thus, all young conversations are monitored by an adult after school and on the weekends, making Ringwood a terrific place for children. All children were transported to and from school by bus, making the transportation department the most essential deliverer of education in the district. Fortunately, I was very sensitive to the issue of school buses from my recent Irvington experience, and was extremely supportive of the needs of that department. Snow, as you would imagine, was a major factor in transporting the children, and snow was a regular visitor to this part of the state. There were a few occasions when we had the bus follow a plow in order to get through the town. In fact, I once had to follow a plow in order to get out of town onto a major road to drive home.

On a Tuesday before Thanksgiving, the weather gurus had forecast a significant amount of snow was to fall in the area on Wednesday. I did my due diligence and checked with other sources, which confirmed the impending precipitation. Being proactive, I announced on Tuesday afternoon that the schools would be closed on Wednesday due to the forecasted snow activity. On Wednesday morning, the only things falling from the sky were bright rays of sunshine.

This was a totally residential community paying approximately $15,000 per year per household in taxes for their schools. There were only a handful of retail outlets in town, including a pharmacy, from which we sadly lost the pharmacist in an automobile accident, a most sad event for the town and for me. VD was my number one informant with regard to the pulse of the community on a variety of issues. One issue in particular, the annual budget vote, was a very big deal. The fact that the budget passed in the Spring of 2001 by ONE vote was a momentous event.

There were numbers of unusual events, possibly typical of a suburban town. A few students, for example, decided to start a rumor about a replication of the Columbine tragedy. A group of adults staged an enactment of a shooting prior to the actual opening of school in the parking lot. There was a scare started by a parent who had just returned from China with her child with respect to the SARS virus; a first grader threatened to bring his father's gun to school for use against a classmate. Speaking of guns,

Ringwood is hunter country. In fact, I believe there were more weapons per capita in suburban Ringwood than there were in urban Irvington.

A teacher at one of the elementary schools had herded a group of 19 students into a small space in order to take a personal telephone call during school hours. In the course of the event, one of the students was burned on the hand by being too close to a radiator. I filed tenure charges for dismissal of this individual as well as suspension of her teaching certificate. The ultimate legal outcome was a suspension with pay, the loss of an annual increment, and reinstatement in her classroom.

Even though the majority of the citizens were quite wealthy, much of my time was spent in discussions about budget, class size, and staff contracts. There were formal meetings, informal forums, special sessions, and even a Saturday morning one-on-one meeting with a board member (GB), complete with coffee and donuts. Communication was the key to my success in this district, and I must report that with the exception of one citizen, the townsfolk were quite cooperative and affable. The aforementioned one citizen was the spouse of my first secretary, whom I had transferred to a school post shortly after my arrival in the district, due to my realization that she was not at all pleased with what my parents may have looked like. "Guess who's coming to be the Superintendent" did not sit well with her at all, or her husband. As time went on, and I worked in Ringwood for five years, the husband reminded his neighbors that Ringwood had a Black school leader, and certainly should not have, in his opinion, and in the opinion of a few others—a very few others.

All of the above pales in comparison in what was going to confront me near the beginning of the 2001-2002 school year. Allow me to share portions of the five memos I penned and sent via fax in a two-hour period:

> TO: Principals/Director
> DATE: September 11, 2001
>
> As you have heard by now, a most unfortunate major tragedy has occurred at the World Trade Center in Manhattan. I shall spare the details as I have monitored them to this time. The Pentagon has also been hit by an airplane.
> . . . .
> Most importantly is that we are sensitive to the fact that there are students whose parents and other loved ones may work in or near to the World Trade Center. Furthermore, we need to avoid PANIC among the children..........
> . . . .
> Our largest concern at this point may be the fact that children whose parents or guardians work in

Manhattan will not be able to get home at the usual time this evening.

Without a doubt, this was the most difficult and challenging day of my career, until I think about the following day. Arrangements were made for food and shelter and supervision in the middle school gymnasium in the event we had to care for parentless children. As it turned out, no parents were lost. Two of the town's young men (in their 20s and 30s) did die in one of the towers. On September 12th, I visited all the children in their schools and classrooms, where one of them asked me the following question: "Mr. Carter, why do other people hate us so much?" I had no answer. Because of the proximity of Ringwood to New York City, fighter jets had been flying over the town all night long, making sound slumber very difficult for the children. The staff and I tried to make the students feel as safe and as comfortable as possible. Let us keep in mind that many of the staff members were parents themselves and lived in other towns. On the 11th, some wanted to leave to be with their own children, and on the 12th, they wanted to stay at home. I strongly reminded them that their number one obligation was to the pupils in their Ringwood classrooms.

Ringwood was blessed with two elementary schools (K-3), an intermediate school (4-5), and a middle school (6-8). The white male principals of these building tolerated, and eventually respected their new black superintendent. I had some help from one of my former Irvington colleagues who came to my rescue as an interim middle school principal. In time, I was even able to hire a female to head one of the schools. All in all, this was an excellent experience! I was ending my New Jersey experience similar to the way it began—in the suburbs with white people. My major accomplishment here was the establishment of the state's first public middle school program for autistic children. We opened the program in a classroom at the middle school with five students—two from Ringwood, and three from neighboring communities.

Sitting at a board meeting on an evening in May, my daughter's words ran through my mind as well as a realization that I did not want to do this anymore. The next morning, I called the Board President and told her of my intention to retire at the end of the school year. She begged me to stay a while longer in order to open schools in the fall. I agreed and changed my retirement date to Halloween of 2004. It was my wish that my retirement function occur in the fire station in town, hosted by the students and parents. It was attended by four former Education Commissioners, former students and their children, dear friends, community leaders, and my daughter. The Board President, also the mother of one of the autistic teens in the aforementioned program, presented me with a Rolex in recognition and appreciation for my services to the children and citizens of Ringwood. The watch has been on my wrist daily.

The local press headline read, "A Long Wonderful Run, Ringwood Schools Chief Wrapping up a Long Varied Career." I was 60 years old. No more need be said (perhaps)!